Driving Complex Change®

Published by *Advanced Solutions in Logistics, Inc.*
Santa Clara, California, USA.

Copyright © 2005 by *Advanced Solutions in Logistics, Inc.*

ASIL, Inc.
2901 Tasman Drive
 Suite 117
Santa Clara, CA 95054
(408) 980-9904;
e-mail: asil-info@asil-inc.com

This publication is designed to provide accurate and authoritative information in regard to the subject matter covered. It is sold with the understanding that the publisher is not engaged in rendering legal or financial services. If legal or financial assistance is required, the services of a competent professional person should be sought.

ISBN: 978-0-9774669-1-7

Library of Congress Catalog Card Number: TX 6-318-223

Library of Congress Cataloging-In-Publication Data: 01/04/2006

Published in electronic format in the United States of America

About the Authors

Peter Pazmany, Michael Vigil and Warren White are senior executives with **Advanced Solutions in Logistics, Inc.** (ASIL, Inc.), a *business performance management* software company dedicated to delivering a suite of proven, performance-driven software solutions applicable to users across a hierarchy of management structures. The heart of this software suite is based upon a new change methodology, **Driving Complex Change®**, which is the focus of this book. All three authors have had extensive operating and executive management experience in functional and business areas within the computer and customer service sectors and across varied domestic and global customer bases.

Peter Pazmany, President and CEO, brings years of well recognized experience in key operational and management roles with **Sun Microsystems, Inc.** and **Hewlett Packard**. He is actively involved with industry and academia on topics such as business performance management, partnering, e-business, and supply chain management. He is an industry expert in developing business performance solutions; streamlining supply chains for the aftermarket business; partnering methodologies and tool sets; building partner networks and integrated solutions; and, process management and performance reporting. Many of the resultant conceptual insights and real time observations drawn from these areas are reflected in the **ASIL Inc.** approach to change management.

Michael Vigil, Executive Vice President of Operations, currently responsible for overall operations and infrastructure within **ASIL, Inc.**, also brings years of operational management experience in the service industry, and, more recently, with **Sun Microsystems, Inc.** to this effort. His involvement in managing partnering efforts, supplier base and inventory pipeline reductions, and organizational ISO9000 certification, and in providing forward looking contributions to industry groups and conferences, coupled with his direct focus on outsourcing, made him a key contributor to the intellectual property embedded in the **ASIL** software product line.

Warren White, Vice President of Change Acceleration Services, an accomplished, award winning senior executive has many years of participative leadership in the service and manufacturing industries for innovative companies such as **Sun Microsystems, Inc., KLA-Tencor, Inc.,** and **Data General Corporation**. His experience in the areas of business transformation and change acceleration range from directing global teams focused on program management and application management for critical business systems management; leading and providing direction to a rapidly growing, supply chain management group for North and South America; to implementing an industry leading partner alliance and collaboration model for significant reductions in spare part program expenditures.

CONTENTS

FOREWORD

SITUATION BEING ADDRESSED

One of the few constants in the world of business is change. At any given time there is little that consistently remains unchanged. Companies face a barrage of internal and external pressures from more demanding customers, stronger competitors, the need for maintaining balanced corporate controls, and shareholders who expect increased value for their investment.

In response to this reality, companies must develop both the capacity to change perpetually within a dynamic business environment and the ability to handle the challenges of change. They must be able to successfully launch fundamental transformations within their organizations, whether this involves entering new markets, expanding product or service lines, or employing new partnering relations. And, they must do so without disrupting their ongoing business operations.

> "The dynamics of our world marketplace today require that we continually be in a process of renewal. However, new systems alone are not the answer. If we simply change from one system to another, this new system soon becomes another box. Instead, we must create a completely new way of thinking-a trail blazing perspective from which we view the present and the future."
>
> -Ed Oakley and Doug Krug[1]

How can a business achieve success while facing these enormous pressures? The actual answer can be found in a couple key areas. A large part of the answer is in the realization that failed projects usually are not flawed in concept but in execution. Typically, change efforts falter because companies fail to communicate effectively with their employees, managers and stakeholders. Some companies do not have their workforce aligned with their core competencies and strategic priorities, companies may lack change plans to guide them through a new strategic business opportunity or operating performance improvement.

To mitigate these execution flaws, companies must improve their ability to navigate through complex change. Successful change results from the up front effort to plan, understand and measure, as well as the enhanced ability to collaborate, communicate and manage the process. Accomplishing this lies in adopting the right approach, tools and delivery critical to success.

> "While virtually everyone understands the need to plan prior to beginning a large-scale, complex project, there is far less understanding of the need to plan how to plan."
>
> - Leonard Goodstein, Timothy Nolan, J. William Pfeiffer[2]

APPROACH TO CHANGE

Although successfully managing a change effort is immediately dependent on what is being changed, the components of change remain largely the same. Recognizing this, we have created a change management methodology, **Driving Complex Change**®, based upon a self-applied diagnostic model coupled with clear and actionable prescriptive feedback. What separates this methodology from other approaches is the inherent simplicity of design and the proven and practical operational elements involved.

This book, in turn, is laid out as a practical guide for the reader to learn, understand and apply the **Driving Complex Change®** concepts for their own change initiative. In the following sections and chapters we will lead you through the conceptual thinking, practical terms, tools, and expected outcomes involved in this methodology; namely through:

- Establishing the business case for the use of the **Driving Complex Change®** methodology;
- Providing an overview of the **Driving Complex Change®** methodology;
- Defining the operational framework for each critical element of this methodology;
- Providing real life examples to demonstrate the application of the **Driving Complex Change®** methodology;
- Supplying helpful insights and advice on how best to apply the **Driving Complex Change®** methodology: and,
- Discussing critical issues and considerations when dealing with complex change.

APPLICABILITY OF METHODOLOGY

The **Driving Complex Change®** methodology is applicable in small businesses, Fortune 500 corporations and all lines of business including financial, manufacturing, service, sales, marketing, supply chain, human resources and information technology sectors. The book itself, is intended for executives, program managers, project teams and department managers who are responsible for leading change programs within their organizations.

DEDICATION

We would like to dedicate this book to our families for their unconditional support and belief in our dreams. Developing a new approach to solving business challenges requires the time to think, create, fail, and try again. Over the past two years our wives – Lisa, Stacy, and Robin have given us an environment in which to experiment and learn. Thank you.

We also want to recognize that a key driving force for our energies comes from our children. So a big thanks to all of our sons and daughters – Peter, Joseph, Stephen, Victoria, Alexis, Aaron, Dimitri, Pamela, Sarah, and Nathan. May all of you be as blessed in the future, as we are in the present.

– Thank you.   Peter, Michael, and Warren

ACKNOWLEDGMENTS

Many people drove the creation of this book. We would like to acknowledge them for their support, ideas, efforts, and commitment to excellence. Each of these folks brought a special value to the overall outcome.

We mentioned our families under the dedication of the book. Quite honestly we can't thank them enough, so thanks again.

We would also like to thank our advisors for their encouragement, insights and belief that we can make a difference in what we chose to do. Thanks – Steve A., Ed, Tom, Steve J., and Dave.

A special level of recognition to our coworkers that helped make this a reality. Their efforts ranged from research to review of materials to the publishing of the final product. Thanks – Aaron Biddle, Alan Bicho, and Debbie LeBaker. A special thanks to Mike Singleton for keeping the show running while we were engaged in this effort.

Finally, thanks to our editor Joe for his insights and willingness to help create the story that shares an alternative for driving business transformations.

All of you have impacted our lives in positive ways and enabled us to dream outside the box.

– Thank you.   *Peter, Michael, and Warren*

PART I

Change and Change Management

In this part....

- Change in the Work Place
- New Change Management Methodology
- Driving Complex Change® Application

In the following chapters 1 through 3, we explore change from a variety of perspectives. Examples include; the dimensions of change, the importance of driving participation and acceptance which improves the effectiveness of the change on business. We'll identify the unique premise behind the Driving Complex Change® methodology and show it's benefits in driving complex change programs. Finally we'll provide an overview of the diagnostic capability and detail the underlying processes and show how the derived information can be used to align and further your strategic programs.

> "Learning to assess the consequences of significant change initiatives is a complex new territory, often neglected by leaders of those change initiatives. In fact, assessment represents an opportunity for those advocating and championing change, particularly for line leaders. If they assume greater responsibility for assessment and measurement of their progress, they can make it a key strategy for accelerating learning."
>
> — Peter Senge, Art Kleiner, Charlotte Roberts, Richard Ross,
> George Roth and Bryan Smith[1]

---

[1] The Dance of Change - The Challenges to Sustaining Momentum in Learning Organizations (Doubleday Publishers, 1999).

Change in the Workplace

Key topics covered in this chapter ....

- Dimensions of Change
- Change Effectiveness
- Change Acceptance
- Change Acceleration
- Organizational Transformation

"Change is the law of life. And those who look only to the past or present are certain to miss the future."

– John F. Kennedy

INTRODUCTION

Change is a constant in the work place. It can come from the introduction of a new project, employees taking on new responsibilities, implementing process improvements, whole scale shifts in the way business is conducted, or the result of a merger or acquisition.

Change is multi-faceted and, as such, has many conflicting dimensions as shown in the following illustration.

Figure 1.1 Multifaceted Paradox of Change

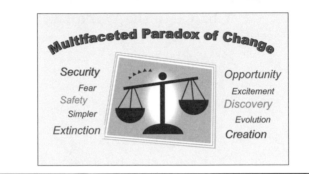

On one hand, change represents opportunities such as productivity improvements, materials cost savings, or more effective alignment to customer requirements. On the other hand, change represents a new way of doing things and thus carries with it a sense of uncertainty that must be addressed for a proposed initiative to be successful.

> "Successful large scale change is a complex affair that happens in eight stages. The flow is this: push urgency up, put together a guiding team, create the vision and strategies, effectively communicate the vision and strategies, remove barriers to action, accomplish short-term wins, keep pushing for wave after wave of change until the work is done, and, finally, create a new culture to make new behavior stick."
>
> – John P. Kotter and Dan S, Cohen[1]

Much has been written on the subject of organizational change and the forces that align to either support or detract, enable or disable, effective and efficient change from being realized. The concepts discussed within this book are based upon the authors' experiences and collaborative feedback. From our first hand observations of applications of these concepts and related methodologies, we have seen how business organizations can accelerate their ability to achieve their change visions, strategies and goals.

---

[1] The Heart of Change (Copyright 2002, John P. Kotter and Deloitte Consulting LLC, Harvard Business School Publishing)

CHANGE EFFECTIVENESS

Organizations seeking to employ a new means to accomplish their business objectives, must consider a variety of factors when determining how best to proceed. Specific characteristics of each objective are important, but the effect of coordinating the implementation of any change initiative within their overall business environment must also be addressed.

We have found that the following basic change effectiveness relationship can be applied to virtually any project, program, product or other initiative, which requires change as part of its development and implementation:

$$Q \times A = E$$

Where;

Q Quality is the design, or functional nature and specific measurable characteristics, of the initiative; that is, a project, product, process or anything tangible that can be expressed as goals, funded and dynamically measured in $, Full Time Equivalents, time or other dimensions.

A Ability is the ability, or agility, of an organization to adopt, accept or advance the practices required for an initiative to be successful and, or, the ability of an organization to actually understand and rally around the specific requirements for the new means to accomplish the work efforts involved.

E Effect is the resultant impact of the change as expressed in the effectiveness or efficiency in productivity or customer value produced.

It is extremely important to understand the change initiative in terms of this relationship. As an example, let us look at its impact in terms of an arithmetic model; namely:

If an organization put 100% into the Q value of the design and 100% into the A value concepts to apply the design then 100% of the E value of the change would be attained.

100% (Q) x 100% (A) = 100% (E) realization of the possible effect of change

Today businesses typically target a Q value around 60-70% and then spend and add resources and time to get to a level of 80%. When they implement, however, the A value is, on average, in the 30-40% range so the range of success, or E value, is in the 24-32% range.

65% (Q) x 35% (A) = 23% (E) realization of the possible effect of change

As you can see, the ability to accept or adopt change can have a significant impact on the overall effect of the change. What would happen if only a marginal investment in change acceptance activity was made on some of the initiatives within your company? Can you see why it is so critical to take steps to manage this ability such that adoption, acceptance and advancement is maximized in your most critical change initiatives?

Let us use the following table to consider some possible combinations of Q and A values and the resulting effects on E values.

Figure 1.3   Change Effectiveness equation combinations 1

Q	A	E
10-20%	80-90%	8-18%
20-30%	70-80%	14-24%
30-40%	60-70%	18-28%
40-50%	50-60%	20-30%
50-60%	40-50%	20-30%
60-70%	30-40%	18-28%
70-80%	20-30%	14-24%
80-90%	10-20%	8-18%

What this table demonstrates is that balancing and applying similar energies in both the Q and A values has the effect of delivering a project, program, product or other change activity with a higher level of impact.

To further illustrate the point, assume that the Quality of the project, program or product has a Q value of 70-80%. Let's now look at the Impact, or E value, from varying energies applied in the area of Ability, or A value.

Figure 1.4   Change Effectiveness equation combinations 2

Q	A	E
70-80%	80-90%	56-72%
70-80%	70-80%	49-64%
70-80%	60-70%	42-56%
70-80%	50-60%	35-48%
70-80%	40-50%	28-40%
70-80%	30-40%	21-32%
70-80%	20-30%	14-24%
70-80%	10-20%	7-16%

In some situations, it would make sense to develop an iterative plan whereby successive versions of the activity are planned, thus increasing the Q value over time. The opportunity in increasing the A value, however, lies in improving time to market.

> "What happens when an organization-however well intentioned-tries to change the structures and processes first? Invariably there is a degree of resistance, usually substantial. Much energy is then wasted on overcoming this resistance to change. This resistance actually negates much of the value of the process changes that are sometimes vitally needed. Yet, the classical approach to change has us first implement system, structure, or process changes to deal with a problem, then expend tremendous energy and resources trying to overcome resistance to the changes, attempting to gain buy-in for them from the people."
>
> – Ed Oakley and Doug Krug[2]

The E value or the effect of change can be measured in terms of time and productivity. Initiatives that have sub-optimal implementation plans can result in lost time, missed deadlines, extended budgets, mistrust and morale degradation and a myriad of other outcomes that cost the company in invested funds, resources and time.

CHANGE ACCEPTANCE

The effects of change on an individual, a team, an organization or a business division can be articulated in a variety of ways. The following graph is a basic illustration of the change acceptance curve, which describes the effect on productivity stemming from a planned or unplanned change in phases over time.

Figure 1.5   Change Acceptance

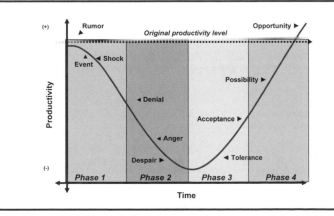

This relationship has been commonly accepted as a relevant model for individuals and organizations faced with significant change driven events or initiatives; that is, change in these cases follows a series of similar phases that can be plotted on a curve showing the effects of either an initiative or event on productivity over time. Business organizations can use this relation to draw meaningful correlations and levels of awareness as well as to develop mitigation methods and means to improve their ability to navigate change.

---

[2] <u>Enlightened Leadership - Getting to the Heart of Change</u> (Fireside Publishers, 1991).

> "While change has been the only constant in our world, the rate of change is accelerating, and organizations that do not anticipate and attempt to manage these rapidly increasing changes face precarious futures."
>
> – Leonard Goodstein, Timothy Nolan and J. William Pfeiffer[3]

A closer examination of the characteristics of each phase depicts a steep decline in productivity before a level of recovery; namely:

Figure 1.6   Phase Characteristics

Phase	Description	Emotional Characteristics	Productivity
1	Rumor and Shock	Uncertainty, inadequacy and overwhelm	Low
2	Denial, Anger and Despair	Confusion, discouraged and helpless	Very Low
3	Tolerance and Acceptance	Peaceful, responsive and pensive	Improving
4	Possibility and Opportunity	Excited, stimulated and energetic	Potential to Exceed

A business manager or executive should care about the change acceptance curve when sponsoring a business change initiative. Why? Because the degree to which the management team understands and leverages the knowledge of the change acceptance curve determines the success of the initiative, the time it takes to complete the implementation of the initiative and the related human, financial and emotional costs.

CHANGE ACCELERATION

Based upon historical evidence, an impacted population will proceed through each phase shown in the change acceptance curve. The time spent within each phase, however, can and will vary depending on the individuals involved, the specific initiative being deployed and the change acceleration methodologies employed.

It is in change acceleration methodologies that businesses have an opportunity to reduce the time and effect of change on the productivity of an impacted organization. Employing the **Driving Complex Change®** methodology, which is discussed at length in this book, can have the effect of accelerating the adoption and advancement of a given change initiative.

Information and knowledge are powerful allies in driving successful change. The methodologies, practices and tools that are part of the **Driving Complex Change®** portfolio enable sustained improvements in both the quality and the ability factors of any initiative. This is accomplished by harnessing information and knowledge and by using these critical areas to make sustainable, repeatable and predictable change.

The objective in employing the **Driving Complex Change®** methodology is to reduce the time it takes to navigate a change and to increase the ability to maximize the capabilities and productivity

---

[3] Applied Strategic Planning - How to Develop a Plan That Really Works (McGraw-Hill Publishers, 1993).

resulting from that change. Example 1, Figure 1.7 , depicts how applying this methodology can improve your ability to navigate and capitalize on a change more quickly; Examples 2, 3, and 4, on the other hand, each reflect extended periods of decreased productivity resulting from sub-optimal change acceptance practices.

Figure 1.7   Effects on productivity after applying change acceleration methodologies

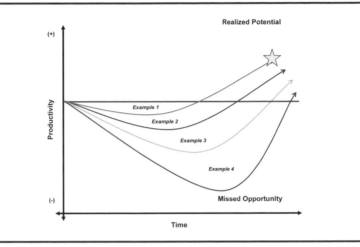

The methods, practices and tools described within this book can also improve the quality of your change program design and your ability to improve the adoption, advancement and acceptance of change. The result will lead to increased productivity and alignment within those organizations or functions required to support the change.

These same methods, practices and tools can enable your business to achieve success by developing the internal capacity to perpetually change within a dynamic environment and be able to handle the challenges of change. The answer lies in your ability to understand that failed projects are not flawed in concept but in execution. Using the appropriate balance of Q and A values will create the effective and efficient business transformations you are seeking.

ORGANIZATIONAL TRANSFORMATION

Change efforts falter because businesses fail to effectively communicate with and manage their employees, managers and stakeholders. They do not align their workforce with their core competencies and strategic priorities nor do they develop change plans that guide the work force along paths to new ways of working.

> "Leaders and constituencies must first acknowledge that what once worked no longer does, and then they must be able to enter into a zone of uncertainty that is at first frightening but from which they emerge reenergized and renewed."
>
> – Jim Kouzes and Barry Posner[4]

---

[4] <u>Credibility: How Leaders Gain and Lost It, Why People Demand It</u> (Jossey-Blass Inc. Publishers, 1993).

To mitigate such execution flaws, businesses must improve their ability to drive complex change. Successful change is the result of planning, understanding and measuring as well as enhancing their ability to collaborate, communicate and manage the processes involved. Accomplishing this lies, in large part, in adopting the right methods for the job.

Business transformation management is a term that denotes a systemic and holistic approach to improving the capacity and capability of a business to drive performance in aligning its vision, strategies, stakeholders, managers and staff within a common integrated management environment.

Successful transformation management solutions deliver reproducible blueprints for driving complex business change. The **Driving Complex Change®** methodology discussed within this book is a business transformation management solution that can deliver that blueprint for success.

Figure 1.8   Effects of applying business transformation techniques

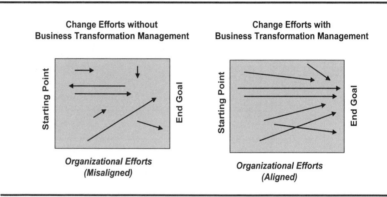

As shown in the above illustration, the left hand graph represents an organization where information about change initiatives is either lacking, ill timed, inconsistent or misaligned. The cost is high. Whether it's failed projects, misunderstood deliverables, ill-timed implementations or competing objectives, the result is lost productivity, wasted resources and stress in internal and external relationships. Most businesses experience this type of change management and never realize the full potential of their effort.

The graph on the right represents an organization where the vision is communicated, enabling the impacted parties to be committed. The individuals involved, individually and collectively, understand their roles and purpose in the change initiative and each team member is pulling their respective weight. This alignment is analogous to all the members in a rowboat rowing in unison towards a common goal. The organization has clarity of purpose and a commitment to execute, which translates into faster adoption and success.

The time proven **Driving Complex Change®** methodology contains a repeatable logical framework that assesses your company's transformation readiness, provides best practice guidance on how to align your organization to the desired change, and then supplies the right performance management solutions to enable effective and efficient business transformations focused on delivering results to the shareholders, customers and stakeholders.

New Change Management Methodology

Key topics covered in this chapter ....

- Driving Complex Change®
- Critical Operating Elements
  - ▪ Direction
  - ▪ Ability
  - ▪ Incentive
  - ▪ Resources
  - ▪ Structure
  - ▪ Action
- Benefits and Expectations
- Impact

"Challenges are what make life interesting; overcoming them is what makes life meaningful."

– Joshua J. Marine

INTRODUCTION

Change, driven by the forces of technological innovation, market dynamics, economic and cultural considerations and the like, consistently occurs within the business world. Companies and organizations must change as well to maintain a competitive advantage and continued viability. Although successfully managing a change effort is immediately dependent on what is being changed, the components of change remain largely the same.

> "Changing behavior is less a matter of giving people analysis to influence their thoughts than helping them to see a truth to influence their feelings"
>
> – John P. Kotter and Dan S, Cohen[1]

There are many, good change management methodologies available to business and technical leaders in today's working environment. Some of these methodologies are comprehensive while others offer specific remedies for very bounded or situational conditions. What separates the **Driving Complex Change®** methodology from these other approaches is the inherent simplicity of design and the proven and practical operational elements.

DRIVING COMPLEX CHANGE® METHODOLOGY

The **Driving Complex Change®** methodology is a set of interrelated and mutually dependent elements, as illustrated in Figure 2.1, for managing successful change. We believe that by understanding and using this methodology to focus in six key areas of a project, program, product or other initiative, you will note a profound impact on the ability of your organization to affect change and, subsequently, your business success. By applying the underlying concepts involved, you will notice remarkable improvements in the areas of quality, the ability to adopt and implement new practices, and overall time to implement. The results will be realized through increased Customer Satisfaction and improved Shareholder Maximization.

---

[1] The Heart of Change (Copyright 2002, John P.Kotter and Deloitte Consulting LLC, Harvard Business School Publishing, Boston, MA).

Figure 2.1   Benefits of Driving Complex Change®

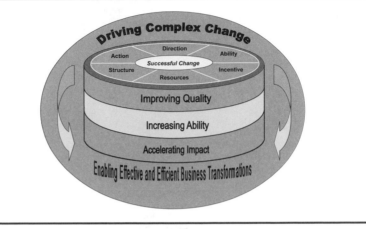

CRITICAL OPERATIONAL ELEMENTS

The **Driving Complex Change®** methodology is based upon the fundamental premise, that by applying rigor and discipline in six specific areas throughout the lifecycle of a specific change, a user can improve the quality, ability and timeliness of that change initiative. The six critical areas, or elements, that we believe must be integrated and managed are direction, ability, incentive, resources, structure and action.

Figure 2.2   Driving Complex Change® Elements

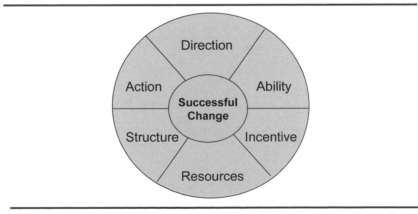

Based upon our experiences and successful outcomes, we have found that when a company or organization understands and drives the requirements necessary for change in these six areas, the opportunity for successful change is increased as much as ten-fold.

The **Driving Complex Change®** methodology takes each of these elements and, using established best practices, analyzes the success criteria requirements and the observed performance in each element. Recommended improvements and actions are then established that will result in that element having a predictable level of success.

To provide an understanding of the focus of each element, the following contrasting descriptions have been included.

DIRECTION

Conventional usage defines direction as "the line or course on which something is moving or is aimed to move or along which something is pointing or facing";

Driving Complex Change® methodology defines direction as "the quality of the vision, strategies, and executive stakeholder support that are critical to the success of any project".

Figure 2.3   Driving Complex Change® - Direction Element

This element is focused on the understanding and readiness of the company in areas such as the value of the business decision, executive stakeholder alignment, a clear value proposition for the customer, the business advantage of completing the change, and, the impact on shareholder value.

Having clear direction for the initiative enables the organization to communicate the attributes of the vision to constituent business units or functions and to create a clear and compelling value for embracing and advancing the change program. Gaps in the area of direction lead to confusion, chaos, misaligned initiatives and, in extreme situations, activities that sabotage the change initiative.

ABILITY

Conventional usage defines ability as "the quality or state of being able; physical, mental, or legal power to perform; the natural aptitude or acquired proficiency";

Driving Complex Change® methodology defines ability as "the cultural, skills, and environmental considerations that must be taken into account for the organization to adopt the new practices required".

Figure 2.4   Driving Complex Change® - Ability Element

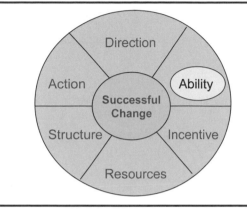

This element is concerned with the evaluation of the skills and capabilities needed to be successful and with the analysis and remediation of any perceived gaps in the current capabilities in these areas. Some of the areas evaluated include core competencies and address whether these core competencies support the new customer value proposition and whether they align with your capital investment strategies.

Having a comprehensive understanding of your ability to adopt and advance the program, enables you to proactively develop your readiness capabilities for successful change. Gaps in the area of ability, lead to stress, feelings of inadequacy, anxiety and resentment.

INCENTIVE

Conventional usage defines incentive as "something that incites or has a tendency to incite to determination or action";

Driving Complex Change® methodology defines incentive as " the availability of programs that drive the behaviors necessary to advance the support and adoption of the change initiative/project".

Figure 2.5   Driving Complex Change® - Incentive Element

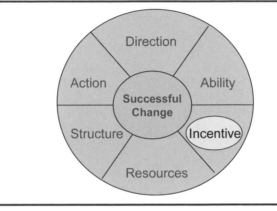

Examples of incentives include the establishment of goals and objectives, measurement and reporting practices, financial systems, reward and recognition programs, and, communication programs.

Maintaining incentive systems that drive the desired behavior are an essential ingredient in creating a successful change program. What you measure, manage and reward matters. Gaps in the area of incentive will manifest into slow adoption, missed opportunities, competing objectives and wasted resource allocations.

RESOURCES

Conventional usage defines resources as "a source of supply or support; an available means";

Driving Complex Change® methodology defines resources as "the appropriate allocation of human, financial and technical capabilities required to complete the required activities needed for a successful outcome".

Figure 2.6   Driving Complex Change® - Resources Element

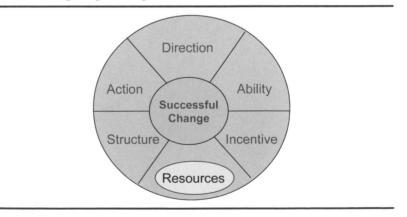

Every change program requires dedicated resources of some kind and level. Resources can range from an executive sponsor, headcount, budget, equipment, software and more. Resource requirements can span across the organization or company as well as be external to both. It is important that you evaluate your resource requirements so that optimum allocations are available for the critical phases of program design, planning, readiness assessment, management, implementation and support.

The allocation and timing of qualified resources to manage and support your program is clearly one of the top contributors to a successful change program. A gap in this area creates poor program design and execution, which leads to frustration and missed expectations.

STRUCTURE

Conventional usage defines structure as "something arranged in a definite pattern of organization; organization of parts as dominated by the general character of the whole";

Driving Complex Change® methodology defines structure as "the elements of a company's business system and their relationship to the predictability of a successful program".

Figure 2.8   Driving Complex Change® - Structure Element

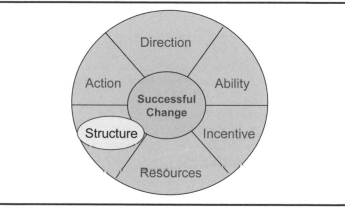

The context for structure includes the overall process, quality, information technology, financial, and other underlying structural elements that comprise the broader business system. Examples of what would be assessed in this area include the organization's preparedness in the area of documented procedures, processes and work instructions, the condition of Service Level Agreements between the operational and supporting organizations, and the ability of the information technology infrastructure to support such considerations as a new Enterprise Resource Planning (ERP) system implementation or provider integration strategy.

Understanding, assessing and managing change in this area is essential to obtaining the return on investment from your program. Without this focus you can easily find yourself developing a great idea only to find an inability to implement. The results would be misallocation of funds, improper use of resources, wasted time, missed opportunities and catastrophic program failure.

ACTION

Conventional usage defines action as "the manner in which a mechanism or instrument operates; the bringing about of an alteration by force or through a natural agency";

Driving Complex Change® methodology defines action as "the overall depth and breadth of the project plan".

Figure 2.9   Driving Complex Change® - Action Element

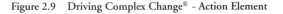

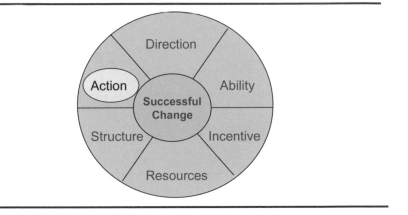

This element addresses a myriad of tactical and operational questions; for example: Is the plan you are embarking on comprehensive enough?   Are the milestones identified and appropriately timed? Have you planned all the actions necessary to be successful and are those actions supported with structures for success? Do you have a contingency plan in place to address shortfalls, gain appropriate management support as needed and is there support for this plan? Have you taken the time to develop the plan and see the way to success?

Change initiatives are fraught with opportunistic shifts. Things that you consider true today are proven untrue tomorrow. What seems easy can become extremely difficult with only a simple turn of events. Can you see your way ahead? Do you have the means to navigate the challenges that will surface?

The action plan is an area sometimes understated but hugely critical to building the confidence and trust needed for support of the change program. Poor focus in developing the plan, communicating the actions required and dealing with the issues at hand will result in missed timelines, increased costs and deteriorating credibility.

Benefits and Expectations

With the **Driving Complex Change®** methodology you get a comprehensive change management system that enables you to focus on the six critical enablers of successful business transformations.

Figure 2.10   Driving Complex Change® Six Critical Elements

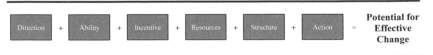

One of the most important benefits of applying the **Driving Complex Change**® methodology is the availability and use of structured questions, observations, recommendations and actions (ORA) stratified by each of the six elements.

By using a series of structured questions and assessing the current state observations from the responses to those questions, the **Driving Complex Change**® methodology is able to assemble and provide recommendations and actions that further increase your program's potential for effective change.

The following overview shows the interrelationships between a given element and the questions, conditions, observations, recommendations and actions.

Figure 2-11   Driving Complex Change® Methodology Overview

Elements	Questions	Conditions	ORA
Direction	Question 1	Absolutely	Observation
	Question 2	Somewhat	
Ability	Question 3	Not Yet	Recommendation
	Question 4	Not Sure	
Incentive	Question 5	Not Required	Actions
Resources			
Structure			
Action			

An additional benefit of the **Driving Complex Change**® methodology is that questions, observations, recommendations and actions can be refined and reused so that your company or organization does not lose the intellectual capital that has been developed. In addition, common policies or acceptable business conduct can be inserted in the direction, ability, incentive, resources, structure and action related questions to drive design and implementation across many of your programs and projects.

Some organizations find themselves using consultants to drive this level of rigor and awareness in program and project management. Adapting and installing the **Driving Complex Change**® methodology provides you with a key differentiator that you do not get by consistently hiring consultants. While hiring consultants can be very beneficial, typically when they are done with a job they then move to another job, taking the intellectual capital developed with them. By utilizing the **Driving Complex Change**® methodology, your organization can effectively build an internal consultant knowledge database which can be leveraged to support future change programs.

Reviewing the focus of the elements of the **Driving Complex Change**® methodology, we can see why it's important to develop the management capacity and ability to view change programs from this perspective. The following illustration shows the effect of deficiencies, shaded in red, in any one element on the potential for effective change.

Figure 2.12   Misaligned Element Negative Impacts

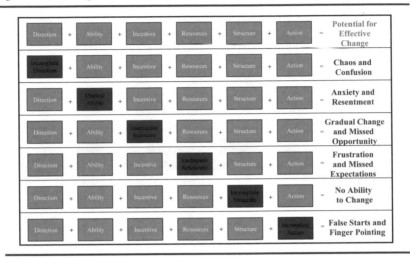

It is clear that a shortfall in any one of these areas can have a negative impact on your overall change program. Typically the shortfall doesn't occur in just one area, but rather in several areas, thus compounding the challenges. It is important to understand gaps in the change readiness condition of your organization and address them as part of a successful outcome.

Think of your change program like the engine of your car; that is, you need all cylinders working together in unison to get where you want to go. Failure of any one or more of your engine components will result in wasted time, lost opportunities, frustration and deteriorating trust.

> "Many people feel especially defensive when someone challenges the way they are doing something-whatever it is. There is a safety factor in doing it their way, the way they've always done it; there is uncertainty in any new way, and the uncertainty threatens their feelings of safety. They feel a loss of control, and being in control is very important to a person."
>
> - Ed Oakley and Doug Krug[2]

Effective, efficient and timely business transformations call for your program to be balanced in the management of the underlying elements - direction, ability, incentive, resources, structure and action.

IMPACT

Now let's look at how applying the **Driving Complex Change®** methodology can make a difference in a typical project.

---

[2] <u>Enlightened Leadership - Getting to the Heart of Change</u> (Fireside Publishers, 1991).

Figure 2.13   Benefits of Driving Complex Change®

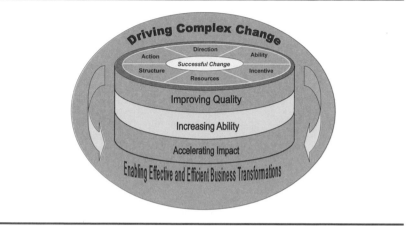

Using the methodology diagram illustrated earlier, we noted that to enable successful change you must remain vigilant in the **direction, ability, incentive, resources, structure,** and **action** areas of the initiative. This requires focus, an integrated planning mechanism, an ability to predict issues and minimize their occurrence, and a portfolio of remedies to address unexpected deficiencies as you proceed with your plan.

Let's illustrate this further within the following working scenario:

Scenario Example

- A new program, called Genesis, has been approved.

- Budget for the program is $12M with program approval for a 6 month lifecycle from design to implementation.

- Projections are that if this program implements at month 6 then the company can capture 80% of the potential market share. Every month delay from that point costs the company 20% of this market share.

- Projected market size for this product is $100M and your existing and potential customers are screaming for it. They want it now whether you, or someone else, can deliver it.

- Resource requirements are for 60 persons of varying skills throughout the program design and implementation phases.

- New skills and capabilities, currently not available within the business, are required and the company must decide to "make" or "buy" these skills as necessary.

- New technologies are also required and a business decision is made to purchase these technologies and install them with the existing information technology infrastructure. This purchase and installation must be completed within 3 months from program implementation.

Let's stop here. Clearly, the program dimensions and constraints cited in this scenario are not unlike some of the characteristics you might face in projects, programs or other initiatives within your business.

Timing is everything in this example. With a run rate of $2M/month and a potential market share loss of 20% per month after month 6, it's clear that any delays would be costly. Failure to implement a quality product on month 6 carries with it a high cost in both Customer Satisfaction and Shareholder Maximization.

Critical questions that must be asked and answered within this program include the following:

- Are the required resources going to be available in the time needed and are they aligned with the importance of this program's success to the business?
- Is it possible that delays in making quality purchasing decisions around new technologies and new skills could delay the program?
- Is it possible that your existing bonus plans and company goals might actually hinder this program from completing on time?
- Are all the actions necessary for completing this program tracked and managed along with other equally important projects and programs within the company to enable Management Executives to make the most timely and appropriate decisions?
- Do other departments within the company know that they are required to support this implementation?
- Do the departments know the support actions required and are they prepared and aligned to do so when needed?

It is in program and project areas like these that the **Driving Complex Change®** methodology goes to work. Applying this methodology enables the breadth and depth of focus required within your business to mitigate and prevent potentially catastrophic failures, and, as a result, maximizes your potential to improve the overall quality, impact and ability to gain results in Customer Satisfaction and Shareholder Maximization.

Using the **Driving Complex Change®** methodology is all about maintaining and advancing the trust and credibility that you and your project or program have worked so hard to create.

Driving Complex Change® - Application

Key topics covered in this chapter ....

- Application Framework
- Diagnostic Questions and Response Conditions
- Observations, Recommendations and Actions
- Expected Benefits
- Next Steps

"The best way to predict the future is to invent it."
- Alan Kay

INTRODUCTION

Although grounded in clear terms and expected outcomes, **Driving Complex Change®** methodology calls for a practical model. To this end, we have created an approach based upon self-applied diagnostics that are coupled with clear and actionable prescriptive feedback.

We will now focus on the application framework for examining each of the six critical elements – direction, ability, incentive, resources, structure and action – within the methodology. Each of these elements will have a set of assigned questions that are designed to assess the status of that particular element.

These questions are based upon a change lifecycle that begins with preparedness for change. This lifecycle focuses on the aspects that must be addressed to create the best potential for effective change. It is important for users to determine how they will address each of the diagnostic questions within the six elements.

DIAGNOSTIC QUESTIONS AND RESPONSE CONDITIONS

Each diagnostic question applied to a given element will have five potential response conditions – Absolutely, Somewhat, Not Yet, Not Sure and Not Required. Users will review the question and then select the appropriate response based upon their knowledge or perception of the situation. Our experiences indicate that the individual responses can be aligned with each of the conditions noted.

A color designator, shown below, is associated with each of these conditions and serves two key purposes; namely:

- To set a range of acceptability for preparedness to change; and,
- To drive the visual outputs to alert management of critical shortfalls or gaps.

Absolutely	
Somewhat	
Not Yet	
Not Sure	
Not Required	

For a given question:

Green designates an **absolutely** condition indicating that you have completed the requisites needed to set the stage for success. This designation would include the ability to demonstrate that this readiness is documented and available for general dissemination; and, would also require the mechanisms to routinely communicate, align, and revise changes within the project or program. Basically, this response suggests that everything is ready to go but it is important that you continue to be vigilant

Light Green designates a **somewhat** condition indicating that you have completed some, if not most, of the change effort requirements but are aware of some gaps in your preparations. These gaps may include a variety of areas that have not been documented or institutionalized and likely will require a series of minor steps to make this condition green. These open-ended items should be addressed on a timely basis to avoid impacting other co-dependent actions.

Yellow designates a **not yet** condition indicating that you have a level of awareness and even a level of intent to take remedial action but, to date, have not taken any material or measurable efforts to move forward. Although future plans may exist, the activities needed to address these open areas are not in place today.

This condition is a stumbling block and can very quickly ramp up your workload. There is also a high likelihood that this will impact the completion of related, serial activities. Resolution of this condition is critical to avoid delays and false starts.

Orange designates a **not sure** condition indicating a lack of user awareness. This is a cause for concern, particularly if the scope of the questions involved are being impacted in some way by the change effort. The sheer ambiguity and uncertainty present make this a dangerous position and will require the user to gain critical perspectives to maintain the proper level of involvement while moving forward. Timeliness is of the essence in this situation.

Red designates a **not required** condition and is typically a red flag item. This response would suggest that the item is not required and the change effort can proceed without further consideration of the area. This conclusion can be very dangerous and requires immediate attention.

The **Driving Complex Change®** methodology is predicated on the relevance of the questions tied to each element of the change lifecycle phase. Although a valid response, the consequences of accepting the **not required** condition without a thorough review for validity can be severe.

OBSERVATIONS, RECOMMENDATIONS AND ACTIONS:

As mentioned earlier, the purpose of this practical diagnostic model is to provide the user with valuable feedback that can be internalized and applied. Based upon the response to a given question and the response condition selected, a series of observations will be provided. The observations, in turn, will define the characteristics needed to successfully address the relative uncertainties raised by the question.

These observations are based upon an integration of real life experiences and collaboration with many companies and academia. They are direct and specific with the goal of providing the user an increased awareness and understanding of both the value in taking action and the steps to drive an effective change.

Directly coupled with each observation is a series of recommendations intended to take the user through the topics that should be considered in moving the effort forward. Each recommendation is focused on those areas and activities within the six underlying elements of the methodology that are most critical to ensuring the best opportunity for successful change. The recommendations could suggest that the user concentrate on confirmation, investigation, re-valuation, standardization and other tasks as a result of this diagnostic process.

The resolution of these recommendations is directly linked to the prescribed actions or detailed steps that must be completed to support a successful change effort. These actions, in and of themselves, will need to have owners and assigned completion dates to provide the framework for measuring progress. Once this framework is completed, a company can enable the foundation that supports this change effort.

EXPECTED BENEFITS

Figure 3.1   Driving Complex Change® Methodology Overview

Elements	Questions	Conditions	ORA
Direction	Question 1	Absolutely	Observation
	Question 2	Somewhat	
Ability	Question 3	Not Yet	Recommendation
	Question 4	Not Sure	
Incentive	Question 5	Not Required	Actions
Resources			
Structure			
Action			

One of the most important benefits of the **Driving Complex Change®** methodology is that *questions, observations, recommendations and actions* can be refined and reused to allow your organization to reuse the intellectual capital that has been developed. You have established a basic framework for assessing the six critical elements of the methodology. The questions that you create to address a given element may be slightly different. What is important, however, is that the questions should hold relevance for your particular purpose and enable you to resolve issues impeding change.

Another important benefit is the value in understanding where you are at a given time and in the clarity on how to move forward in a predictable and sustainable manner. This will facilitate your ability to assess progress, understand the broader issues involved, and take the necessary corrective actions. Longer term, the ability of you and your company to consistently and successfully navigate any change will be strengthened.

With one integrated snapshot, management can visualize problem areas and themes and quickly assess where their focus should be applied and how to realign efforts. At a more operational level, the methodology can also be utilized to compare and contrast different responses for the same effort from different groups or functions. This helps the program or project team understand differences in perceptions that could negatively impact the program

A company must always weigh the need to employ a different way of doing business versus the cost and trade-offs involved. The objective is to enable companies to build and maintain their intellectual capital, to develop a routine way to reuse their knowledge, and finally, to implement change successfully.

NEXT STEPS

This chapter has set the stage for the practical demonstration of the **Driving Complex Change®** methodology. Subsequent chapters will enable the user to become familiar with the challenges of change and the related tools available to resolve and move their project forward. Chapter 4 will begin with a practical focus on the element of Direction.

PART II

Driving Complex Change®
Concepts, Methods and Practices

In this part....

- • Driving Complex Change® Methodology
  - ◻ Direction
  - ◻ Ability
  - ◻ Incentive
  - ◻ Resources
  - ◻ Structure
  - ◻ Action

In the following chapters 4 through 9, we will outline and demonstrate the interrelated and mutually dependent elements and operational tools of the **Driving Complex Change®** methodology with practical user applications. You will find that, in this methodology, we have created an integrated change management approach based upon self-applied diagnostics coupled with actionable prescriptive feedback and grounded in clear terms and expected outcomes to implement and adopt change.

> "While change has been the only constant in our world, the rate of change is accelerating, and organizations that do not anticipate and attempt to manage these rapidly increasing changes face precarious futures."
>
> − Leonard Goodstein, Timothy Nolan, J. William Pfeiffer [1]

---

[1] <u>Applied Strategic Planning - How to Develop a Plan That Really Works</u> (McGraw-Hill Publishers, 1993)

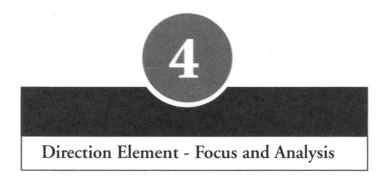

Direction Element - Focus and Analysis

Key topics covered in this chapter ....

- Direction Element
  - Current State Assessment
  - Future State Development

- Assessment Impact and Change Implementation

INTRODUCTION

To this point we have discussed the need for change management methodology in terms of change effectiveness and acceptance and organizational or business transformation. We have also defined **Driving Complex Change®** methodology in terms of change management success and the related application of a practical assessment framework focused on the underlying elements – direction, ability, incentive resources, structure and action – and self-applied diagnostics and actionable feedback. This standardized, controlled approach utilizes a series of questions to guide you through a step-by-step analysis of your area of focus. These questions assess the current state, design the future state, and provide controlled practices to close gaps and reduce risks.

DIRECTION - ASSESSMENT, OBSERVATIONS, RECOMMENDATIONS AND ACTIONS

Earlier we defined direction as "the quality of the vision, strategies and executive stakeholder support". We will now identify the key assessment questions that are a part of this element and why they are important. Once defined, we will then review each question against a selected condition in order to address the observations, recommendations and actions (ORA) presented. Each question will include a listing of support tools and processes that can be applied to any exposed areas.

CURRENT STATE ASSESSMENT – KEY QUESTIONS AND ASSESSMENTS

We have developed the following set of pertinent questions that focus on ensuring that this element – direction – is prepared to support a major change effort:

Do you have Executive Stakeholder alignment and support?

Executive Stakeholder alignment and support are critical to any major change effort. Alignment means that you have agreement with the direction of your change project and support means that management will help to ensure that your project receives the organizational and financial resources to succeed. These stakeholders are management champions for your change project and, as such, are your escalation point for major issues and roadblocks.

> "The reactions of stakeholders to [a project's] perceived impact can be sudden and disruptive if not thought through in advance."
>
> – Leonard Goodstein, Timothy Nolan, and J. William Pfeiffer[1]

If you do not have Executive Stakeholder alignment and support, you may soon find that you no longer have the required resources or prioritization necessary to be successful.

> "Successful change is rooted in commitment. Unless key participants in a transition are committed to both attaining the goals of the change and paying the price those goals entail, the project will ultimately fail. In fact most change failures trace back to this lack of commitment, with obvious symptoms like sponsors terminating projects or more subtle signs such as target apathy serving as leading indicators."
>
> – Daryl R. Conner[2]

---

[1] Applied Strategic Planning - How to Develop a Plan That Really Works (McGraw-Hill Publishers, 1993).

[2] Managing At The Speed Of Change - How Resilient Managers Succeed and Prosper Where Others Fail (Villard Books Publishers 1992).

Do you have a cross-functional team to lead this effort?

A cross-functional team, made up of representatives of organizations impacted by the change effort and key support functions, is important for success. Having this representation in place ensures that action items associated with these functional areas will be addressed and enables a vested interest in your project.

Without this team in place, eventually an issue will arise in a non-included support area that may have to be escalated to management level for resolution. Because this area will not have been part of the team and have no visibility or awareness of the issue, they will have no support reserved for your change project. This will cause delays and frustration to occur.

> "When people are preparing themselves for change, the key issues are "What will happen?" "When?" and "How will it affect me?" Answering these questions decreases ambiguity, reduces anxiety, and restores a measure of control - although the pain of transition will still exist. People have such a deep need for control that being able to anticipate and understand even negative change can be regarded as a source of comfort."
>
> - Daryl R. Conner[3]

Will this decision increase shareholder value?

With any major change effort, the question as to whether it increases shareholder value should be asked. Every major change effort should have a return on investments to the shareholder. Whether it improves Customer quality, lowers costs, increases efficiency or other performance measures, all of these examples positively impact shareholder value in one-way or another.

If your change project decreases shareholder value, then why is it being done? Somewhere down the road there must be a positive impact for the shareholder and this question makes sure that you have taken that impact into account.

Do you have agreed upon vision and strategies defined to support change?

Vision defines the end state that you are driving for and strategies define how you are going to get there. The end state vision is important because you want to know when you cross the finish line. Strategies are important because you need to outline how you will achieve the end state. You can modify your strategies as you progress; however, these changes only improve the road map for moving forward to the desired end state.

If vision and strategies are not defined, then the scope of your project could continually change, causing your program to grow beyond the planned end state and drift from its original intent.

> "One way to gain alignment within the company is to provide people with data and information about markets, customers, and industry benchmarks that are directly related to the company's plan."
>
> - Daryl R. Conner[4]

Do your strategies map to your Customer Value Proposition?

Your Customer Value Proposition (CVP) is tied to the basic reason for the existence of your company or organization. It includes a thorough understanding of the core competencies being provided to your customer and defines your strengths and how they will be invested to achieve a competitive advantage. It is important that your strategies map to and support your CVP; it will be difficult to

---

[3] Managing At The Speed Of Change - How Resilient Managers Succeed and Prosper Where Others Fail (Villard Books Publishers, 1992).

[4] Leading at the Speed of Growth (Copyright 2001, Kauffman Center for Entrepreneurial Leadership, Ewing Marion Kauffman Foundation, Published by Hungry Minds Inc., New York).

achieve your business objectives if they do not.

> "When it comes to improving quality, customer service, productivity, sales, and all the other hard issues, we must recognize that people only apply themselves to the degree that they see the value of what they are doing. This sense of values grows out of their perception of the worthiness of the organization's purpose or mission and of how what they do contributes to that mission."
>
> – Ed Oakley and Doug Krug[5]

Future State Development – Observations, Recommendations and Actions

We will now focus on applying the six elements as they pertain to a hypothetical situation. The following scenario will become the foundation upon which we will review all six critical elements of **Driving Complex Change®**. This will establish the starting point for the change effort and will define the known aspects of the case.

Pertinent questions will be addressed and the results evaluated to ensure that your team has the greatest potential for a successful change effort. Each chapter will explore the issues related to achieving success as they pertain to one of the six critical elements. Questions will be focused on ensuring that the element being reviewed is positioned for success. Based upon the user's response to said questions, specific observations, recommendations, actions, and support tools will be defined to resolve the open challenges.

We will begin in this chapter with **direction**, and proceed through the other elements in the subsequent chapters. Chapter 10 will bring all of the learning together to create a concise review of the lessons learned and value gained.

---

[5] Enlightened Leadership - Getting to the Heart of Change (Fireside Publishers, 1991).

Scenario Example

"You have been designated as the Program Manager of a major restructuring effort within your company (ABC). In addition, ABC has just completed the acquisition of another company (XYZ) and this effort will require integration of the newly acquired company into the current organizational structure. There are many stakeholders involved, some of whom are not in synch with the changes proposed.

Product alignments, central to this acquisition, are solid, but there are clear cultural and operating style differences between the two organizations. Communications about this restructuring effort have been spotty and, as may be expected, many rumors have been circulating about job cuts and big changes. All this had led to levels of fear and uncertainty as to how individuals and functions will be impacted.

This project will include outsourcing of specific functions that are not considered core competencies within the restructured company. Competencies to be retained or strengthened will need to be agreed upon and, in non-core areas; plans for divestment of those activities need to be developed.

You are currently on a small team that has HR and Finance members. Functions within ABC are unsure of what is required of them and whether they have the resources to meet the rumored time lines.

Existing business practices have been partially documented and distributed, however, some undocumented practices do exist. There are also questions about the overall readiness of these practices to be moved to an outside provider. The processes involved will need to be institutionalized and measured to determine if the restructuring objectives and goals are being achieved.

Executive Management is expecting a game plan that ensures that a smooth, timely and successful organizational integration and related outsourcing effort. A variety of e-mails have been exchanged between the management teams of both companies and expectations are currently unbounded. This lack of aligned focus within the teams makes building a restructuring plan for management approval and funding difficult."

There are questions in the element of **direction** that you need to ask as well as answers to evaluate to ensure that your team can be successful. The following is a look at five questions that should be asked in this scenario, the condition that exists in relation to each question and **observations**, recommendations and actions, which should be followed.

Question 1 Do you have Executive Stakeholder alignment?

Condition:	Absolutely	Somewhat	Not Yet	Not Sure	Not Required

Observations: Your feedback suggests that this is an area yet to be addressed. It sounds like you have the intention, and you now need to move forward to make it happen. Depending upon how far along you are on this project, this could be an area of exposure. Alignment and support of the executive stakeholders is critical to the success of your change project.

Executive Stakeholders are those persons who have a vested stake in the outcome of the action being taken. They may be part of the team delivering support or a direct part of the change project. Gaining their alignment and support is tied to a few key elements, which include the following:

- Determine the Executive Stakeholders;
- Defined and agreed upon Vision;
- Defined and agreed upon Strategies;
- Defined and agreed upon Plan and Budget;
- Clear communication and reporting channels; and,
- Understood measurement for success.

By ensuring that each of these areas is established, the overall success of the change project will increase measurably.

Recommendation: Your follow-up should stress building and maintaining credibility for your project through adherence to these critical elements; namely:

- Ensure that you determine and then meet with the correct Executive Stakeholders.
- Establish Executive Stakeholder alignment and gain their support.
- Communicate the results to stakeholders, project team members, and support organizations.
- Upon resolution, continue to update Executive Stakeholders on a periodic basis.
- Ensure that your project plan milestones and time line reflect the added time necessary to complete this activity.
- Ensure that the sign off process is closely adhered to.
- Ensure that cost is tracked and measured against planned spend.
- Ensure that the communication plan covers all parties impacted.

Actions: Detailed steps that provide a framework for measuring and reporting progress to your Executive Stakeholders are directly linked to resolution of these recommendations. These steps, as shown below in a flow-charted form, allow

Figure 4-1 Question 1 Action plan

stakeholders to directly track progress within the restructuring effort.

Support Tools   A *Stakeholder Assessment* is one of the fundamental tools of any sound Change Management practice. The Stakeholder Assessment tool allows for the following areas to be analyzed:

- Understanding the impacted populations for a given organizational change;
- Assessing the business population to determine what group support is essential to advance a proposed business change;
- Understanding the stakeholders with the most impact on the success or failure of the business change;
- Assessing different opinions or concerns within groups on the relevance of a given change;
- Developing and assigning appropriate actions to address the concerns of the affected populations; and,
- Developing a mindful and methodical approach to transforming the understanding of the proposed change within business constituents to advance the change effort in an effective and efficient way.

By completing a Stakeholder Assessment, you will be able to identify any areas of concerns among your stakeholders. This enables you to not only monitor their actions, but to put in place a plan to either get them on board to support your project or take actions to mitigate the risk of not having their support.

Question 2 Do you have a cross-functional team to lead this effort?

Condition:	Absolutely	Somewhat	Not Yet	Not Sure	Not Required

Observations: Based upon your feedback your intention is to move forward with a cross-functional team. Depending upon how far along you are on this effort, this could be an area of exposure to your change project. It is critical to have a broad team that incorporates a variety of disciplines and perspectives.

We have found that teams that have cross-functional representation deliver timelier results in a more predictable fashion. Cross-functional team membership could include the following high level functions:

- Operations/Business
- Finance
- Human Resources
- Legal
- Information Technology
- Program Management

Each function supporting the process being changed must participate in the project. Otherwise, critical functions will not be able to support the effort being called upon.

Recommendation: With these observations in mind, taking the following recommendations will ensure that key functions are on board and aligned with the operational plans, budgets, functional requirements and time lines are critical to project success:

- Ensure that you develop a list of required cross-functional participants.
- Enlist support of Executive Stakeholders to help ensure that the team is seen as important and is supported.
- Agree on the team protocol and operating parameters once the correct parties have been identified, empowered, and signed-up.
- Enlist all parties to address issues and opportunities.
- Distribute meeting minutes and action items.
- Ensure that your project plan milestones and time line reflect the activity required to put this in place.

Actions: A sequential approach, as shown below in a flow charted form, is important in defining and justifying cross-functional team requirements to your Executive Stakeholders and in enabling development of a commonly held appreciation of project operating plans and team structures.

Figure 4-2 Question 2 Action plan

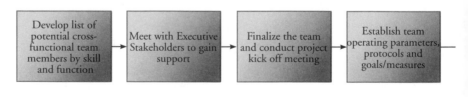

Support Tools   Utilizing the results of the *Stakeholder Assessment*, as discussed in Question 1, to ensure that each critical stakeholder will have a representative on the project team is one of the fundamental elements of any sound Change Management practice.

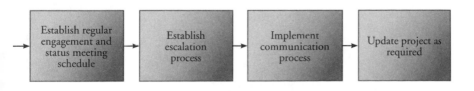

Question 3 Will this decision increase shareholder value?

Condition:	Absolutely	Somewhat	Not Yet	Not Sure	Not Required

Observations: Caution,

Your feedback suggests that this area has yet to be resolved. This could be an area of exposure to your change project. Either there is a time delay that may or may not be known, and/or there could be a follow on effort that completes the picture and will drive shareholder value. If there is a time delay that will take place before shareholder value is achieved, then it is important to document the timing of when the value should arrive and track it until it is delivered. Over the course of time, you may have to reassess the shareholder value received.

Driving customer satisfaction is critical and must be done while achieving maximum profitability. Shareholders today expect more than ever before. They want to know that their interests are always coming first.

Recommendation: As with any major change effort, expectations related to the positive impact on shareholder value should be addressed early on and re-enforced periodically throughout that effort. This should include the following:

- Establish a review to understand the complete expected impact on the stakeholder.
    - If impact is minimal and not clear why you would want to proceed, reprioritize effort as "nice to do".
    - If there is a time delay, ensure that you document the expected time line to achieve shareholder value, and monitor progress and reassess as necessary.
    - If impact is sizable then continue to understand business trade-offs.
- Work with Finance to ensure that the financial goals and objectives are being addressed and measured; and,
- Advise Executive Stakeholders of determinations and go forward actions.

Actions: Action steps, as shown below in a flow-chart, allow you to answer questions on the areas of impact on stakeholder value and how and when they will be realized.

Support Tools: *Return On Investment* (ROI) is a return ratio that compares the net benefits verses total costs of a project. As such, ROI is a measurement of operating performance and efficiency in utilizing assets by a company. With a ROI in place, you can determine the size of the benefit to the company, how long it will take for benefits to be realized and where the benefits will occur.

Figure 4-3 Question 3 Action plan

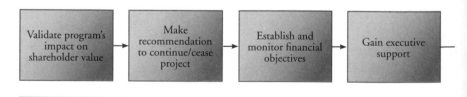

Typically an ROI is required up front for major projects like acquisitions in order to validate the projected benefits of the acquisition. Your Finance organization plays a large role in the development, approval and support of an ROI. Once completed, it is not placed on a shelf and forgotten, but utilized instead as a reference to validate that the company is realizing the expected benefits.

| Establish regular project/shareholder value alignment review | → | Regularly review and communicate alignment of customer/shareholder value | → | Report periodically to Executive Stakeholders on customer/shareholder value |

Question 4 Do you have an agreed upon vision and strategies defined to support change?

Condition: Absolutely   Somewhat   Not Yet   Not Sure   Not Required

Observations: This could be an area of exposure to your project. Your feedback suggests that you are unsure if an agreed upon vision and strategy are in place.

It is critical that the Executives have a common understanding of the vision to achieve the related strategies; otherwise, there will be many missed expectations. This will be due to the lack of a clear understanding of the projects objectives. The vision should be about the future and something that people can rally around; the strategies should be the approaches to be taken to achieve the vision. Ultimately, the combination of the two is designed to create a competitive business advantage.

This element will also enable the cross-functional team to progress into the planning and implementation phases, which re-enforces the criticality that the project vision and strategies have support and approval at the Executive Stakeholder level.

Recommendation: Take steps to ensure that the scope of your project is defined in terms of your anticipated end state or vision and strategies for getting there; namely:

- Meet with Executive Stakeholders to confirm or establish the vision and strategies for the change effort and, upon agreement, assess the current situation and determine where the gaps exist:
- Resolve gaps and drive for resolution with Executive Stakeholders and, upon final agreement, continue to update them over time;
- Ensure that the vision and strategies that support change are communicated to other stakeholders, project team members and support organizations.
- Monitor the progress of the strategies to ensure that the vision is still in focus.
- Perform periodic calibration to ensure that the vision still fits, and the strategies are still correct.

Figure 4-4 Question 4 Action plan

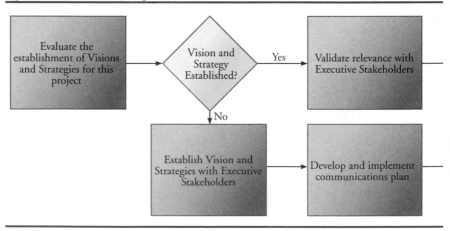

Actions: An iterative approach, as shown below in flow charted-form, will allow you to not only define your vision and strategies with your Executive Stakeholders but also to address decisions on strategy changes as you progress.

Support Tools: *Envision the Future Tool* assists business executives in establishing a strategic framework for significant success. The framework consists of the following:

- A vision that the organization is driving to;
- A mission that defines what you are doing;
- Values that shape your actions;
- Strategies that zero in on your key success approaches; and,
- Goals and Key Performance Indicators (KPIs) to guide and measure your daily, weekly and monthly actions.

These concepts ultimately provide direction for an organization and allow it to pursue activities that lead the organization forward, thus avoiding the misappropriation or misdirection of critical resources. In essence, the success of your organization and your personal success depend on how well you define and live by each of these important concepts.

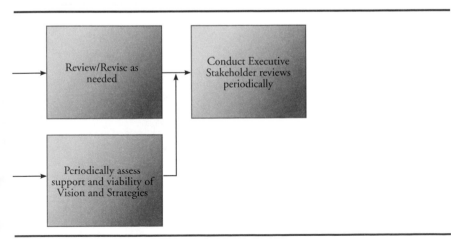

Question 5 Do your strategies map to your Customer Value Proposition?

Condition:	Absolutely	Somewhat	Not Yet	Not Sure	Not Required

Observations: Caution.

Your feedback suggests that it is not required to map your project strategies to your Customer Value Proposition (CVP). This may be true for a variety of reasons. Most likely, the effort has no direct impact on the customer or perhaps it is a back office transaction. However, if this is directly related or has an impact on a customer, we encourage you to seriously reconsider and take the steps needed to gain alignment.

Your Customer Value Proposition is tied to the basic reason for the existence of your company or organization. It includes a thorough understanding of the core competencies being provided to your customer and defines your strengths and how they will be invested to achieve a competitive advantage.

It may be difficult to achieve business objectives if proposed investments are not supportive of either CVP or Shareholder Value Proposition (SVP). The mapping process is not overly time consuming and should be performed in order to avert major problems downstream.

Recommendation: Ensure that you determine whether your strategies need to align with your CVP. If not, then move forward with the project and communicate regularly with stakeholders; conversely, if yes, then you must address the following:

- Ensure that you meet with executive stakeholders to map your current strategies to your CVP.
- Determine gaps and revise the strategies with the executive stakeholders.
- Ensure that the revised strategies are communicated to stakeholders, project team members and support organizations.
- Ensure that you continue to monitor the revised strategies to ensure

Figure 4-5 Question 5 Action plan

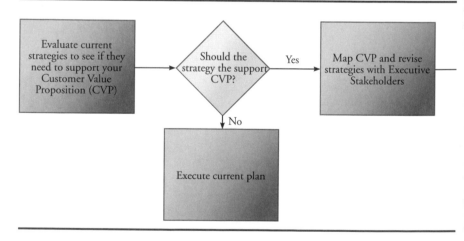

that they continue to map to your CVP.

- Ensure that a forum is in place to assess and resolve any future gaps between the strategies and the Customer.
- Ensure that those involved in the project understand the Customer Value Proposition. This will help them to understand the desired end result.

Actions: If needed, an approach, as shown below in flow charted-form, will allow you to map out, align and communicate your Customer Value Proposition and provide an iterative process to address changes in strategy as you progress.

Support Tools: *Envision the Future Tool* assists business executives in establishing a strategic framework for significant success. The framework consists of the following:

- A vision that the organization is driving to;
- A mission that defines what you are doing;
- Values that shape your actions;
- Strategies that zero in on your key success approaches; and,
- Goals and Key Performance Indicators (KPIs) to guide and measure your daily, weekly and monthly actions.

These concepts ultimately provide direction for an organization and allow it to pursue activities that lead the organization forward thus avoiding the misappropriation or misdirection of critical resources. In essence, the success of your organization and your personal success depend on how well you define and live by each of these important concepts.

ASSESSMENT IMPACT AND CHANGE IMPLEMENTATION

Depending upon the project you are leading, there may be other outcomes in the area of direction, which must be assessed. The opportunity to add additional questions, which provide more insight and greater preparation, is always an available option. Unique projects may require focused attention in the area of government approval or support, corporate policy changes, legal ramifications or financial considerations to name a few. These areas may require their own questions that must be assessed to ensure a successful change effort.

Once you have completed your assessment in the **Driving Complex Change®** element of direction, you will know whether you are on solid ground and where you should focus resources in order to be able to support a successful change effort. Expected outcomes include the following:

- Understanding the business value
- Executive Stakeholder alignment
- Customer Value Proposition defined
- Team makeup identified
- Business advantages captured
- Shareholder Value defined

By ensuring that key aspects of **direction** are in place, you have enabled a key element which supports the successful implementation of complex change within your organization or company.

Ability Element - Focus and Analysis

Key topics covered in this chapter ....

- Ability Element
  - Current State Assessment
  - Future State Development
- Assessment Impact and Change Implementation

"An organization's ability to learn, and translate that learning into action rapidly, is the ultimate competitive advantage."

– Jack Welch

Introduction

We have defined **Driving Complex Change®** methodology in terms of change management success and the related application of a practical assessment framework focused on the underlying elements – direction, ability, incentive resources, structure and action – and self-applied diagnostics and actionable feedback. We have reviewed the standardized, controlled approach and utilized a series of questions in the area of direction to guide the user through a step-by-step analysis. These questions assess the current state, design the future state, and provide controlled practices to close gaps and reduce risks. We will now move through another set of questions in the element of ability.

Ability - Assessment, Observations, Recommendations and Actions

Earlier we defined ability as "the cultural, skills, and environmental considerations that must be taken into account for the organization to adopt the new practices required". We will now identify the key assessment questions that are a part of this element and why they are important. With that in place, we will then review each question against a selected condition in order to address the observations, recommendations and actions (ORA) presented. Each question will also include a listing of support tools and processes that can be applied to any exposures.

Current State Assessment – Key Questions and Assessments

We have developed the following set of pertinent questions that focus on ensuring that this element – ability – is prepared to support a major change effort:

Do you have a process to understand and identify your core competencies?

Understanding and identifying your core competencies is a critical requirement for management to be able to make effective business decisions and set strategy. When management understands their company's core competencies, they can then develop more sharply defined investment and disinvestment strategies.

> "The habits that have led to your initial success are especially difficult to break. It's hard to fathom that the very behavior that contributed to your success at one stage can cause you to stall out or fail at the next. But it can, and it will."
>
> – Katherine Catlin and Jana Matthews[1]

By having a standardized process to determine their core competencies, a company can improve upon the process as they move through iterations of understanding and identifying those competencies.

> "There are multiple ways to close the gap between the organization's current state and its desired future state. Generally, these options will fall into either a growth or a retrenchment category, depending on the relationship of the current organization and its desired future."
>
> – Leonard Goodstein, Timothy Nolan, and J. William Pfeiffer[2]

[1] Learning at the Speed of Growth (Hungry Minds, Inc. Publishers, 2001).

[2] Applied Strategic Planning - How to Develop a Plan That Really Works (McGraw-Hill Publishers, 1993).

Do your core competencies support your Customer Value Proposition?

This question is a check of whether you have mapped your identified core competencies to your Customer Value Proposition. If your core competencies do not support the value your company delivers to its Customers, then is it really a core competency? This question also checks whether a company understands and has identified its Customer Value Proposition. Many times this is assumed, and upon further investigation and understanding, the Customer Value Proposition is different than what was assumed.

> "When your organization's activities are tightly aligned to its intentions-when its projects (and structure) deliver on what it's trying to achieve-the portfolio is more coherent and unified, which means less organizational friction at all levels. And when there is less internal friction, people and systems simply perform better.."
>
> – Cathleen Benko and F. Warren McFarlan[3]

Are your non-core competency areas well-defined and measured for results?

It is important that non-core competency areas be well defined and have established measurements in order to be able to outsource these areas. If a non-core competency area is not well defined or measured, then it is difficult to outsource effectively. How will you be able to explain what work needs to be done and within what parameters? How will you measure the performance of a new partner? To outsource effectively, you must understand and have established metrics for any function that is to be transitioned to a partner.

Do your core competencies tie to your capital investment strategies?

Once you understand and have identified your core competencies, then the question is: "Are you investing in these core competencies?" If you are not, then your company could lose the competitive advantage it has established in these areas. It is important to continually improve and grow in core competency areas in order to stay ahead of the competition.

Do you have an outsourcing plan for your non-core competency areas?

Does your company have a strategy to develop an outsourcing plan for identified non-core competency areas? If it doesn't, it should. By outsourcing those functions which do not provide a competitive advantage, your company is able to leverage highly skilled companies who have developed best practices within these functions. These companies continually invest in these functions, whereas your company will not. This enables your management team to focus on and invest in strategic core competency areas.

FUTURE STATE DEVELOPMENT – OBSERVATIONS, RECOMMENDATIONS AND ACTIONS

We will now focus on the element of ability as it pertains to the scenario we established in Chapter 4. The following is a brief outline of our scenario, with some additional focus on this element.

---

[3] Connecting the Dots - Aligning Projects with Objectives in Unpredictable Times (Harvard Business School Publishing, 2003).

Scenario Example

"You have been designated as the Program Manager of a major restructuring effort within your company (ABC). In addition, ABC has just completed the acquisition of another company."

"This effort has many stakeholders and will require the integration of the new company (XYZ) into current organization within ABC."

"This project will include outsourcing specific functions not considered core competencies; and, core competencies will need to be agreed upon and plans for disinvestment will need to be developed."

"Existing business practices are partially documented and distributed; yet there is much risk in the undocumented practices and in the readiness to move them to an outsourced provider. The processes will need to be institutionalized and measured to determine if the restructuring objectives and goals are being achieved."

"Your project team's current focus is on outsourcing opportunities. Your company has a standardized process for identifying core competencies and has run through this process with the XYZ functions."

"Your company has not redefined the newly merged company's Customer Value Proposition but your team feels that they know it. Non-core competency areas are not well defined or measured for results. In addition, your team is unaware of an investment strategy that supports core competency areas. Your company does not establish outsourcing plans based upon the results of identifying non-core competency areas."

There are questions in the element of ability that you need to ask as well as answers to evaluate to ensure that your team can be successful. The following is a look at five questions that should be asked in this scenario; the condition that exists in relation to each question; and, the observations, recommendations and actions that should be followed.

---

[1] *Enlightened Leadership - Getting to the Heart of Change (Fireside Publishers, 1991).*

Question 1 Do you have a process to understand and identify your core competencies?

| Condition: | Absolutely | Somewhat | Not Yet | Not Sure | Not Required |

Observations: Excellent!

Your feedback suggests that you have a process to analyze and review the core competencies within your company. With this type of knowledge, your project is on the right track.

Core competencies, simply defined, are areas where your company will make focused internal investments in order to gain or maintain a competitive advantage.

The basic steps in a core competency review process include:

- Defining the Customer Value Proposition (CVP)
- Reviewing existing resources for alignment to CVP
- Determine desired future state
- Develop a gap assessment and investment plan
- Develop a plan to disinvest in non-core competency areas
- Create a change management plan

Recommendation: Your follow-up should focus on building and maintaining the process capability to define and balance your core competencies and related resource requirements against your Customer Value Proposition over time; that is:

- Ensure that your analysis process includes executive signoff, weighted critical factors that map to your CVP, prioritization, qualitative and quantitative analysis, financial analysis and is documented as a repeatable process.
- Ensure that you reassess your CVP to ensure that your core competencies have not changed.
- Ensure that your knowledge of core and non-core competencies guide your capital investments.
- Ensure that your disinvestment plan for your non-core competencies has executive management approval and is reviewed and updated regularly.
- Ensure that your change management plan maps your core and non-core competencies.
- Ensure your core and non-core processes are measurable.

Actions: A staged approach, as shown below in flow-charted form, that will allow you to periodically evaluate your Customer Value Proposition and determine what

Figure 5-1 Question 1 Action plan

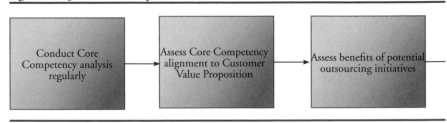

Conduct Core Competency analysis regularly → Assess Core Competency alignment to Customer Value Proposition → Assess benefits of potential outsourcing initiatives

adjustments to your core competency areas and resource commitments may be required.

Support Tools: A *core competency evaluation* provides business executives with a structured, easy means to assess the value of various business functions and, once assessed, to determine the appropriate level and type of investments required for a given business function. This is critical to ensure that a company is divesting (i.e. outsourcing) and investing in the appropriate areas.

When a company participates in outsourcing, it can be a difficult process determining which function or process to outsource because it impacts employees and management who currently work for the company. It is important that a core competency evaluation occur in order to take a great deal of the emotion and angst out of the decision making process.

A core competency evaluation can be accomplished as part of an annual renewal of goals and strategies or it can be used as an on demand analysis tool.

Question 2 Do your Core Competencies support your Customer Value Proposition?

Condition: Absolutely   Somewhat   Not Yet   Not Sure   Not Required

Observations: Based upon your feedback, this could be an area of exposure. It is extremely important that you have an established and agreed upon process that aligns your core competencies to your Customer Value Proposition (CVP).

The CVP is the foundation for your company's inherent deliverable. It defines what you will provide to a customer in exchange for monetary and other considerations.

> "Capabilities do not produce economic value by themselves-they have to be put to use in a productive activity. They have to be allocated to a project and consciously combined with other resources. Over time, every valuable capability will need to be upgraded through investments of capital and effort. All these activities require managerial decisions, and so are shaped by the structure of control in the organization. Control over a set of capabilities thus determines how these capabilities will be used and developed over time."
>
> – Benjamin Gomes-Casseres[4]

Recommendation: With these observations in mind, taking the following steps to ensure that core competency areas are not only defined but also aligned to your Customer Value Proposition is critical:

- Ensure that you map your core competencies to your CVP.
- Ensure that the gaps that are found are reviewed, and action taken if necessary to close the gaps.
- Ensure that you regularly review your core competencies to affirm that they have not changed.
- Ensure that you regularly validate your CVP.

Actions: An approach, as shown below in flow-charted form, will allow you to contrast and affirm or adjust your core competency alignments to your Customer Value Proposition.

Support Tools: *Customer Value Proposition* (CVP) is a technique, which articulates the differentiation for each target customer segment. It is a sharp definition of the value the company creates for its target customers; that is, what it offers; the unique benefits, which nobody else offers; the costs to the customer of attaining these benefits; and, the trade-offs the customer must make in choosing one

Figure 5-2 Question 2 Action plan

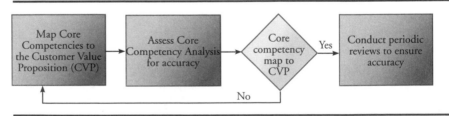

---

[4] The Alliance Revolution - The New Shape of Business Rivalry (First Harvard University Press 1996).

supplier over another.

It is not a marketing slogan, but a clear focus for the whole business; that is, what it does inside and what it delivers outside. Winning organizations must give customers a reason to choose them. They must stand out from the crowd through differentiation that is relevant and meaningful to the target customers.
There are five main considerations when setting your CVP; namely:

- *Customers* -- Who are the best target customers or markets?
- *Theme* -- What is the essence of our offering to them - the central idea?
- *Unique Benefits* -- What is the unique benefit that differentiates us from our competitors? What additional benefit differentiates us from our competitors?
- *Pricing* -- What is our relative price position in the marketplace?
- *Trade-Off* -- What will customers not get when they choose us?

Surprisingly, a recent survey showed that only 32% of companies believe they have clear differentiation in their marketplace. This is an astonishing fact, implying that the others are satisfied at playing as commodities in a parity world.

As an example the Co-operative Bank has chosen to differentiate itself by being "more ethical" than its competitors. This provides the bank with a distinctive marketing message, but also has implications for how the whole company does business. SAS Hotels has a similarly strong differentiation, by being the "most environmentally friendly" hotel. They do not necessarily seek to be the most comfortable or the most luxurious hotel, but they are distinctive in a way, which matters to their target customers.

Question 3 Are your non-core competent areas well defined and measured for results?

Condition:	Absolutely	Somewhat	Not Yet	Not Sure	Not Required

Observations: Caution.

Your feedback suggests that your non-core competency areas are not well defined and that performance measures may not be adequate. This could be an area of exposure. By not having well defined measurements in place you risk making the wrong outsourcing Provider selection decisions and establishing a relationship that does not improve performance over time.

Non-core competency areas are those that do not have to be completed in house due to any legal requirements; that your company is not planning on making any investments in moving forward; and/or, that can done by external Providers in a more consistent and focused manner. As an example, today you may ship your own products, however, you are not a distribution company so you are not investing in the latest distribution technology. There are many distribution companies that are solely focused on distribution who are making these investments and, most likely, will be able to improve on your existing distribution processes and technology.

Measuring the results of your non-core competent areas means that you understand and measure the Key Performance Indicators (KPIs), which reflect productivity and efficiency. You should have over 12 measurement periods (typically monthly) at a minimum in place to be able to set goals and contractual requirements for an outsourced Provider.

Recommendation: Take the following steps to define your non-core competency areas and related performance measurement requirements. This is a critical part of provider selection and contract decisions when outsourcing functions or processes.

- Identify your company's non-core competent areas.
- Use this information to compare your non-core competent functions to the industry experts of those functions to support your outsourcing decision-making.
- Establish well defined measures for your non-core competent areas.
- Use these performance metrics to establish the contractual performance requirements and to measure ongoing performance of the outsourced Provider.
- Continue to reassess your core competent areas as you successfully outsource functions and processes. It is common for companies that outsource effectively to redefine their core competencies over time and to expand their outsourcing opportunities.

Figure 5-3 Question 3 Action plan

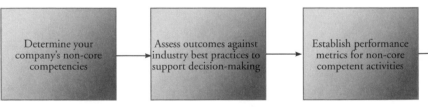

- Ensure that your project plan includes any additional milestones and time required to understand your non-core competent areas and establish performance metrics.

Actions: A staged approach, as shown below in flow-charted form, will allow you to determine your non-core competency functions and define performance and metrics expectations as precursors to setting contractual performance requirements for an outsource provider.

Support Tools   A core competency evaluation provides business executives with a structured, and easy, means to assess the value of various business functions and, once assessed, to determine the appropriate level and type of investments required for the given business function.

The main focus pulled from a core competency review is the identification of non-core competency areas, which are likely candidates for outsourcing. Non-core competency areas typically are not receiving investments in order to stay up to date with the latest technologies and methodologies. They can be outsourced to a company who specializes in this area for all of their customers. The cost of their investments is spread across their customer base so that no one company carries the burden of the investment. They are also focused on every aspect of the function, whereas your company is focused on core competency areas. Costs should lower, while quality, efficiency and performance should increase when outsourcing a non-core competency area.

The *Process Management Tool* is used to describe the current characteristics of a process, a managed sequence of steps, tasks, or activities that converts inputs to an output. By documenting the processes, the Provider will be able to understand how success was being achieved and then evaluate how their core competencies can successfully integrate into these processes; and in turn, enabling them to:

- Simplify or improve the processes;
- Achieve the same results and performance initially, then increase results
- Return financial benefit to the company.

By utilizing the structured framework of the Process Management Tool, you will describe the process steps, criteria or metrics used, desired improvements, and work instructions that are currently being used for each of the processes. These details will be the groundwork for analyzing potential providers. The more detail that is provided; the more accurate your evaluation will be.

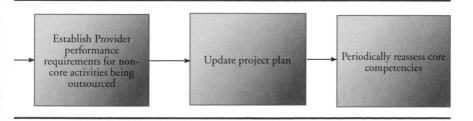

Question 4 Do your core competencies tie to your capital investment strategies?

Condition:	Absolutely	Somewhat	Not Yet	Not Sure	Not Required

Observations: Caution.

Your feedback suggests that you are unsure whether your core competency areas are tied to your capital investment strategies. By not having these capital investment decisions understood, your company may well be investing in the wrong areas. Investments may be made in non-core competency areas while core competency areas are overlooked. If this is occurring, then your core competency areas will fall behind and no longer be a competitive advantage.

Every company has to decide where they are going to make their investments. Many times, this is done by what appears to be the greatest need, not necessarily considering the areas the company has designated as core competency areas. When a company does not invest in their core competency areas, they tend to fall behind in technology in those areas, losing productivity and competitive advantage. By accounting for the core competency areas while in the budget planning stages, it will help to ensure that these areas are not missed during the allocation process. Core competency areas require continual investments in order to deliver a sustained competitive advantage.

Recommendation: Ensure that your core competency areas are mapped and are part of the capital investment strategies, which leads to the budget allocation process, to ensure continued investment. Budget allocations to fix any gaps found during this mapping process will require executive management and finance approval.

If your company is investing in core competent areas by default and not via a process accounting for core competencies, then you should update or initiate a process that does account for core competencies as part of developing your company's capital investment strategies

Actions: A framework is shown below in flow-charted form to facilitate your ability to review your core competencies and your capital investment strategies.

Figure 5-4 Question 4 Action plan

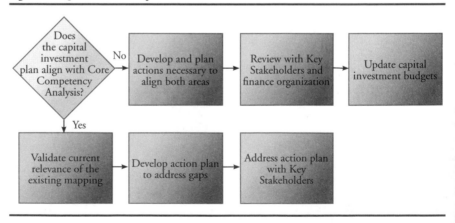

Support Tools   A core competency evaluation provides business executives with an easy, structured means to assess the value of various business functions and, once assessed, to determine the appropriate level and type of investments required for a given business function. This is critical to ensure that a company is investing and disinvesting in the appropriate areas.

Once you have completed a core competency evaluation, if you find that your capital investments are not tied to your identified core competency areas, then you need to review whether these really are your core competency areas. Core competencies require continued investment in order to ensure that your company builds and maintains a competitive advantage.

Question 5 Do you have an outsourcing plan for your non-core competent areas?

Condition: Absolutely   Somewhat   Not Yet   Not Sure   Not Required

Observations: Your feedback indicates that your company may not be taking advantage of an opportunity to outsource non-core competency areas. There could be many possible advantages to developing an outsourcing plan, which may include but are not limited to:

- Identifying non-core competency areas
- Investing only in core competency areas
- Outsourcing to gain financial benefit
- Outsourcing to improve performance
- Outsourcing to improve Customer Satisfaction
- Outsourcing to gain a competitive advantage

This is a decision that you should make as a company. By developing an outsourcing plan for non-core competency areas, your company can focus and invest in those areas which deliver a competitive advantage.

It is important that every company clearly define the areas that are core competencies and those that are not. Those that are, should have continued investments made in them to ensure that they provide the company a sustained competitive advantage. Those that are not should be considered for outsourcing because the company does not plan to invest in these areas.

An outsourcing plan outlines the core competency areas of the company and then prioritizes which areas should be outsourced first by using financial gain, increased productivity, improved Customer Satisfaction, and enabled competitive advantage, as the key decision criteria.

Recommendation: Assess if your company needs to develop an outsourcing plan for non-core competency areas; and,

Figure 5-5 Question 5 Action plan

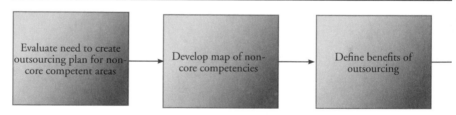

Evaluate need to create outsourcing plan for non-core competent areas → Develop map of non-core competencies → Define benefits of outsourcing

- If no, ensure that executive management understands the possible opportunities that exist in order to revisit this decision in the future;

- If yes, then:

  - Identify non-core competency areas.
  - Gain executive management support of outsourcing non-core competency areas.
  - Ensure that an outsourcing plan is developed based upon the feedback
    from executive management.
  - Ensure that the key stakeholders approve the new outsourcing plan, which should include the following areas:

    - Stakeholder approval
    - Approved resources
    - Communication plan
    - Change management plan
    - Competency analysis
    - Financial analysis
    - Comprehensive prioritization
    - Selection process

Actions: A framework, as shown below in flow-charted form, allows you to evaluate the need for an outsourcing plan for non-core competency areas and, if needed, to map out and define a plan for key management and stakeholder approval and funding.

As was noted for Question 4, a core competency evaluation provides business executives with an easy, structured means to assess the value of various business functions and, once assessed, to determine the appropriate level and type of investments required for a given business function.

An outsourcing plan utilizes the information from the core competency evaluation to identify outsourcing candidates. These candidates are then prioritized to determine which ones will provide the greatest positive impact

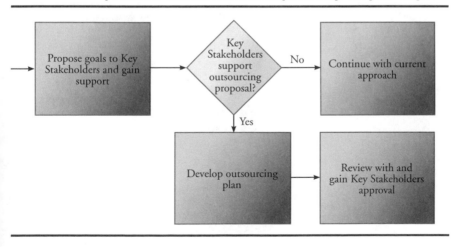

for the company. Key factors in this process include:

- Cost reduction
- Quality improvement
- Performance and efficiency improvement
- Increased scalability
- Improved information technology
- Implementation of best of breed methodologies
- Movement from a fixed cost model to a variable cost model

These and other benefits must be identified to determine the prioritization of your outsourcing plan. For each project or process to be outsourced, you must have a detailed project plan to move any project or process from in-house to an external provider.

ASSESSMENT IMPACT AND CHANGE IMPLEMENTATION

Depending upon the project you are leading, there may be other outcomes in the area of **ability** that must be assessed. The opportunity to add additional questions, which provide more insight and involve more preparation, is always an available option. Unique projects may require focused attention in the area of government approval or support, corporate policy changes, legal ramifications or financial considerations, to name a few. Areas like these may require their own questions that, in turn, must be assessed to ensure a successful change effort.

Once you have completed your assessment in the **Driving Complex Change**® element of ability, you will understand your strengths as well as those areas that need increased focus to successfully effect change.   Expected outcomes include the following:

- Understanding your core competencies
- Identifying non-core competent areas
- Understanding if your core competencies support your Customer Value Proposition
- Understanding if your core competencies tie to your capital investment strategies
- Identifying if an outsourcing plan exists and is valid

By ensuring that key aspects of ability are in place, you have enabled a key element which supports successful implementation of complex change within your organization or company.

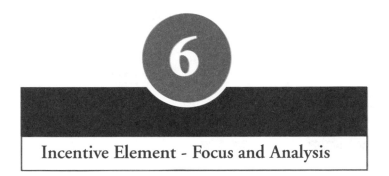

Incentive Element - Focus and Analysis

Key topics covered in this chapter ....

- Incentive Element
  - Current State Assessment
  - Future State Development
- Assessment Impact and Change Implementation

"For every company, every boardroom in which I sit, has a plan, and they have objectives, goals and a process. And to make it work, the pressure and incentive as to come from the top."

- Vernon Jordan

INTRODUCTION

We have defined **Driving Complex Change®** methodology in terms of change management success and the related application of a practical assessment framework focused on the underlying elements – direction, ability, incentive resources, structure and action – and self-applied diagnostics and actionable feedback.   We have reviewed the standardized, controlled approach and utilized a series of questions in the areas of **direction** and **ability** to guide the user through a step-by-step analysis. These questions assess the current state, design the future state, and provide controlled practices to close gaps and reduce risks. We will now move through another set of questions in the element of **incentive.**

INCENTIVE - ASSESSMENT, OBSERVATIONS, RECOMMENDATIONS AND ACTIONS

Earlier we defined **incentive** as *"the availability of programs that drive the behaviors necessary to advance the support and adoption of the change initiative/project"*. We will now identify the key assessment questions that are a part of this element and why they are important. With that in place, we will then review each question against a selected condition in order to address the **observations, recommendations** and **actions** (ORA) presented. Each question will also include a listing of support tools and processes that can be applied to any exposures.

CURRENT STATE ASSESSMENT – KEY QUESTIONS AND ASSESSMENTS

We have developed the following set of pertinent questions that focus on ensuring that this element – **incentive** – is prepared to support a major change effort:

Have you defined the goals and objectives for this effort?

By establishing goals and objectives for your change effort, you have set the targets that must be achieved in order to reach your goal. Management can approve the resources required in order to achieve these goals and objectives; progress can be tracked and reported; and, communications can be planned and established to inform employees of program expectations, targets and progress. Goals and objectives set the basis for resource approval, project tracking, communications and more.

Are these goals and objectives measurable and achievable?

Goals and objectives that are not measurable are subjective in nature and not clear as to when they have been achieved. If goals and objectives are set that are measurable but not achievable, then the project has been set up for failure from the start. For these reasons, it is important that all goals and objectives are both measurable and achievable.

Do you have an internal rewards system in place to support desired outcomes?

Companies that have an established internal reward system, which is focused on desired outcomes, have been very successful. When employees have a specific goal, which is tied to a reward of some type, teamwork and focus are improved. Employees are more apt to help one another to ensure that the goal is achieved and the reward can be received. It is also important that the reward is set on goals that stretch their capability, not something that can be easily achieved.

Do you have a predictable and sustainable measurement and reporting process?

Measurement and reporting processes are critical to measuring performance and progress. Key Performance Indicators (KPIs) can be established which measure individual and team performance. These same KPIs provide the basis for reporting to management. Your measurement and reporting process must be predictable and consistent. It must also be sustainable, continually maintained and improved when necessary.

Do you have an external rewards system in place to support desired outcomes?

External reward systems provide an extra incentive to Providers who wish to differentiate themselves from their competitors, and keep them in focus for any new opportunities, which may arise. Common external rewards systems are relatively inexpensive to manage, and usually involve the presentation of a trophy or plaque to the selected Provider, which is kept in the company office listing all past winners.

Typically these are awarded every quarter after Performance Scorecards have been completed. The award is best presented in front of the entire Provider base. The recognition for the Provider is greatly enhanced, and other Providers will want to be on the stage for the next presentation the following quarter, driving them to improve their efficiency, productivity, delivery and quality.

FUTURE STATE DEVELOPMENT – OBSERVATIONS, RECOMMENDATIONS AND ACTIONS

We will now focus on the element of incentive as it pertains to the scenario we established in Chapter 4. As a reminder, a brief outline of our scenario, with some additional focus on this element, is shown below.

Scenario Example

"You have been designated as the Program Manager of a major restructuring effort within your company (ABC). ABC has just completed the acquisition of another company."

"This effort has many stakeholders and will require the integration of the new company (XYZ) into current organization within ABC."

"This project will include outsourcing specific functions not considered core competencies; and, core competencies will need to be agreed upon, and plans for disinvestment will need to be developed."

"Existing business practices are partially documented and distributed, yet there is much risk in the undocumented practices and in the readiness to move them to an outsourced provider. The processes will need to be institutionalized and measured to determine if the restructuring objectives and goals are being achieved."

"Your project team's current focus is on ensuring that the project is well defined and that the right incentives are in place to support the integration of the two companies. Your team has defined the goals and objectives for the integration, however, some of the goals and objectives are subjective."

"No bonus program has been established to support the completion of this project, but there is consensus that this needs to be put in place. Your team is unclear as to the current state of the measurement and reporting process. There is no plan to put in place a rewards program for any of your external providers."

There are questions in the element of **incentive** that you need to ask and response to evaluate to in order to ensure that your team can be successful. The following is a look at five questions that should be asked in this scenario; the condition that exists in relation to each question; and, **observations, recommendations** and actions that should be followed.

Question 1: Have you defined the goals and objectives for this effort?

Condition: | Absolutely | Somewhat | Not Yet | Not Sure | Not Required

Observations: Excellent.

Your feedback suggests that you have defined goals and objectives for your change project. The core team must be aligned with key stakeholders' expectations. Clearly defined goals and objectives allow for responsibility and accountability for all levels of management on your project. Ensure that goals are set using *SMART* guidelines; that is, they are – Specific, Measured, Achievable, Realistic, and Time Based.

Recommendation: Your follow-up should stress building and maintaining credibility and alignment with key stakeholders for your project goals and objectives: namely:

- Ensure that you have clearly defined goals and objectives for all levels of management assigned to the project.
- Ensure that the goals and objectives are aligned with key stakeholder expectations.
- Ensure that any modifications to project goals and objectives are clearly communicated and adopted.

Action: A framework, as shown below in flow-charted form, will allow you to develop and align your project plan with Key Stakeholder expectations.

Support Tools: The following tools are useful in developing the desired results in this area. Consider applying these tools, or their underlying principles, when driving improvements in this area.

Envision the Future Tool assists business executives in establishing a strategic framework for success. This framework consists of the following:

- A vision that the organization is driving towards into;
- A mission that defines what you are doing;
- Values that shape your actions;
- Strategies that zero in on your key success approaches; and,
- Goals and Key Performance Indicators (KPIs) to guide and measure your daily, weekly and monthly actions.

Identifying the goals and KPIs that must be established to measure success is extremely important to completing your project as planned.

Figure 6-1 Question 1 Action plan

> "When your organization's activities are tightly aligned to its intentions-when its projects (and structure) deliver on what it's trying to achieve-the portfolio is more coherent and unified, which means less organizational friction at all levels. And when there is less internal friction, people and systems simply perform better."
>
> – Cathleen Benko and F. Warren McFarlan[1]

A *Project Management Tool* consolidates all the actionable records (those with delivery dates) into one centralized area. This allows for a common monitoring point as well as a single area for reporting of actionable records. The actionable records within Project Management Tool are organized by date and by status of the deliverable. Typically project management tools use an easy-to-view stoplight configuration; this is, Red being for overdue records, Yellow being within 7 days of due date, and Green for on track records. This tri-colored graphical summary makes it easier to determine the status of projects and to quickly identify the owner of those projects.

Employing a Stakeholder Assessment mechanism may prove useful as well. When defining strategies, goals and objectives it is critical that these goals are adopted by all those who must be engaged to drive their progress. Using the Stakeholder Assessment Tool allows you to identify all the entities that must be involved to promote and drive the attainment of a specific goal.

---

[1] Connecting the Dots - Aligning Projects with Objectives in Unpredictable Times (Harvard Business School Publishing, 2003).

Question 2: Are these goals and objectives measurable and achievable?

Condition: Absolutely   Somewhat   Not Yet   Not Sure   Not Required

Observations: Based upon your feedback, this could be an area of exposure. It is extremely important that you have measurable and achievable goals and objectives for your change project. Executive Management must believe that the measurement system can track to their desired outcomes. Your performance metrics must be realistically achievable and reported on a timely basis to your key stakeholders. Ensure that your project goals follow the *SMART* guidelines; that is, they are – Specific, Measured, Achievable, Realistic and Time Based.

Recommendation: With these observations in mind, taking the following steps to ensure that project goals and objectives can be measured and tracked over time is critical to building commitment within your project team and support with your key stakeholders:

- Establish an understanding with the core team that goals and objectives are specific and measurable in nature.
- Ensure that goals and objectives are realistic expectations that can be achieved by the core team's efforts
- Review measurement systems and project performance metrics.
- Ensure that timely reporting is aligned with goals and objectives.
- Ensure that measurement systems are aligned.

Action: An approach, shown below in flow-charted form, will allow you to communicate and gain acceptance that your project goals and objectives are achievable and measurable with key stakeholders.

Support Tools: *SMART* is a term that is use to describe a method of setting, documenting, measuring and achieving goals that results in goals that have the attributes of being Specific – Measurable – Achievable – Realistic and Timed Based.

These five components provide a solid foundation for goal setting. Whenever

Figure 6-2 Question 2 Action plan

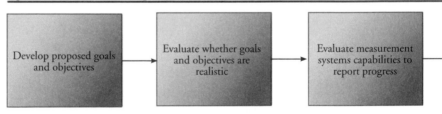

you are going to set a goal, you should compare the proposed goal to these components to ensure that it measures up. *SMART* components are defined as follows:

- **Specific** - A goal needs to be exact, distinct and clearly stated. Vague generalities are not goals and will not enable you to successfully achieve your desired end state.
- **Measurable** - How do you know when the goal is completed? When specifying the goal, you should state how you are going to measure its completion. It is always best to be working with mature metrics that have trending data available. If the measurement system is vague or subjective, then completion of the goal could be suspect.
- **Achievable** - Ensuring that a goal is achievable is extremely important. It must be attainable and questions such as, "Am I in control of all the variables?" and, "Do I need anything else that I do not currently have to achieve this goal?" should be answered.
- **Realistic** - Setting a realistic goal is fundamental. While many goals may be achievable, they may not be realistic. If, for example, your company has merged with several companies this past year and a goal was set to utilize only one financial system for all of these merged companies this first year, is this achievable? Yes, if you invested heavily in your own manpower, external consultants, and the entire focus of your IT departments on this goal. Typically, this is not realistic, especially in one year. Just determining which financial software is best to use for your company could take one year. So be sure that your goal that is set is realistic.
- **Time Based** - You need to ensure that your goal is time based and continually addressing when it will be achieved. Many times goals have sub goals, which measure specific milestones to ensure that you are on track and to offer the chance to celebrate success. This helps reinforce the importance of these sub goals to team members driving toward the overall goal.

Write it down. You should keep a written record of the goal so there is no doubt in your mind what it is. You should have a log of how you arrived at that particular goal. It will also be useful to tick off goals achieved to highlight difficulties as well as to improve on your goal specification based upon what you

Propose goals to Key Stakeholders, identify gaps, risks, and gain support

have learned about yourself along the way.

There are other behavioral and motivational factors to consider when establishing goals; that is, goals should express and be the following:

- **Positive** - State a goal using positive language. Avoid words such as "but" and "not".
- **Compatible** - The goal has to be compatible with all your other goals as well as those of others that may be directly affected by its successful completion. Is it compatible with your team or organization goals? Is it legally, ethically or environmentally compatible with society?
- **Challenging** - The right degree of challenge is a motivator. You do not want to set goals that are easily achieved. Everyone supporting the goal can easily see that this goal does not stretch your organization and therefore could question the integrity of the goal setting process. Ensure that, when you achieve the goal, your organization has reached new heights, had to stretch your team, and increased your knowledge.
- **Commitment** - Ensure that you and your team are committed to the goals. Constant communication of the goals by providing updates and addressing challenges are ways to ensure that your team stays committed to the goals.
- **Rewarding** - It is important to understand what the rewards are for achieving the goal. Will your company be more successful? Will the Customer be more satisfied? Will it save the company money? Will the workforce gain more knowledge? These are some of the questions to be answered. It is also important to establish rewards for the participants wherever possible. Is there a possible pay raise or bonus for achieving the goal? Does it enhance future career advancement?
- **Understood** - Particularly important in a team environment where many people may have decided on the goals, is to be sure the goals are not open to misinterpretation.

This is an iterative process, ensuring that all the conditions are met. This may mean revisiting each goal. Once completed you will have formulated a worthwhile goal. This will maximize your chances of success and lead to the desired future state. It is also important for you to review both the long term goal successes and failures along the way and to make appropriate changes from the lessons learned.

Completing a Stakeholder Assessment may prove useful as well when defining goals and objectives, particularly to ensure that they are attainable. Using the Stakeholder Assessment Tool allows you to assess all the stakeholders that must be involved to promote and drive the attainment of a specific goal and those who must provide support to ensure that you can objectively measure a goal. Once you've identified the teams that must be involved you can use the Stakeholder Assessment Tool to identify current levels of support, desired levels of support required, specific issues and concerns that exist, and what specific actions could be utilized to drive acceptance and support in those groups.

Question 3: Do you have an internal rewards system in place to support desired outcomes?

Condition: Absolutely   Somewhat   Not Yet   Not Sure   Not Required

Observations: Your feedback suggests that you do not have an internal rewards system in place to support desired outcomes. This could be an area of exposure.

An internal reward system can range from the employer's annual performance review, spot bonus', and/or a specific reward program for the project. The latter is typically used on major project across company initiatives (i.e. implementation of a new financial software application). It is critical to success that individuals and groups assigned to the project commit and support the desired outcomes as defined by *SMART* goals and objectives. An internal rewards and recognition system will ensure their commitment and support to your change project.

Recommendation: Project and support team expectations of an internal rewards and recognition system tied to project outcomes should be addressed early on and re-enforced periodically throughout the change effort; that is:

- Gain an understanding with key stakeholders and Finance to ensure that funding and approvals are in place for an internal rewards system.
- Ensure that the rewards system in place is consistent and objective.
- Ensure that internal rewards system is aligned with your desired outcome.
- Ensure internal rewards system is tied to *SMART* goals and objectives.

Action: An approach, as shown below in flow-charted form, will allow you to develop and gain approval for an internal rewards system for your project with key functions and stakeholders.

Support Tools: A rewards system that is designed specifically to support specific goals and objectives can be an extremely effective motivation tool for your employees. It is important that the Key Performance Indicators are well defined, documented, and communicated. This enables your employee base to continually focus on performance and to monitor progress to ensure that they meet and beat the required KPI levels to receive their reward.

Typically this reward is monetary based upon level of compensation. If, for example, the required KPI levels are met, all employees who directly supported the performance will receive a 2% bonus. Usually management is exempt

Figure 6-3 Question 3 Action plan

from these bonus programs because they already have a separate bonus program in place.

In order to establish an incentive bonus program like this, a budget must be approved by Finance and Human Resources to ensure that there are no conflicts with other employees or programs. Of utmost importance, is to ensure that there is no way to game the system in order to achieve the bonus. Constant monitoring and auditing are required to minimize this possibility. This type of bonus program galvanizes the workforce to achieve the goal, generates new ideas to address problem areas, and drives employees to step up into leadership roles.

Question 4: Do you have a predictable and sustainable measurement and reporting process?

Condition: Absolutely   Somewhat   Not Yet   Not Sure   Not Required

Observations: Caution.

Your feedback suggests that you are unaware of whether you have predictable and sustainable measurement and reports process in place to track the performance of the function or process targeted for change. Depending on your specific situation, this could be a significant exposure area.

If your project calls for another group or company to take over the entire process or function and perform the work utilizing their own processes and systems then, in this instance, there would likely not be a major issue. If you felt that your measurement and report systems were not reliable and you wanted the new support structure to develop new baselines, then this would likely not be an issue as well.

In both cases, you would want to ensure that you work with a team that is highly skilled in the process or functional area. If, however, you are planning on measuring the current performance measures against what will be delivered in the future, you will have to determine what metrics and reports you have in place now, are they adequate, and should more be developed.

Recommendation: With these observations in mind, your follow-up should stress building both an understanding of your current and projected measurement and reporting system and the credibility that the system with requisite changes will support expected project outcomes. The following steps should be taken:

- Determine what measurements and reporting processes must be put in place today to measure the process or function being targeted for change.
- Ensure that your measurement and reporting processes maintain the predictability and sustainability of your KPIs.
- Establish a management alert process for when sub-optimal performance is reported by your measurement system.
- Understand what gaps exist in measurement and reporting, validate their level of importance, and establish an action plan to initiate critical

Figure 6-4 Question 4 Action plan

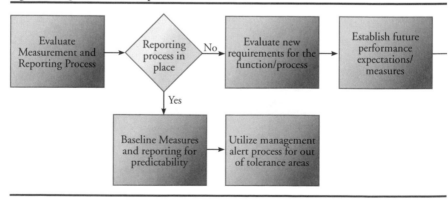

metrics and reports changes.

- Update your project plan and timeline to account for any additional time required to establish new metrics and reports.

Actions:

- A framework, as shown below in flow-charted form, will allow you to evaluate your current measurement and reporting system, and define and gain approval for changes to bring the system in line with future measurement and performance expectations.

Support Tools

- A *SWOT* (Strengths, Weaknesses, Opportunities, and Threats) *Analysis Tool* allows business executives to assess their current organization or organizational plan from a viewpoint that considers organizational strengths, weaknesses, opportunities and threats. Typically these SWOT analyses are accomplished during an annual business planning cycle, however, they could just as easily be carried out at any time for Executive Management.

- A SWOT analysis would also be useful in understanding the current state of your measurement and reporting process. You can identify where the strengths and weaknesses of the current measurements and reporting; the opportunities that are available to improve measurement and reporting capability; and, finally, what threats are in place which could inhibit establishing those improvements.

- Employing a robust *Communication Plan* can go far in driving improvements in this critical area. The reporting process for goals does not apply simply to a specific goal but also to the overarching adoption and advancement of the efforts required to attain that goal. Taking the time up-front to assess the parties required to advance the efforts and to determine the communications required to align their efforts as well as the type of communications and frequency of communications required to achieve a goal is time well spent. Don't underestimate the power of communication when it comes to achieving your critical goals.

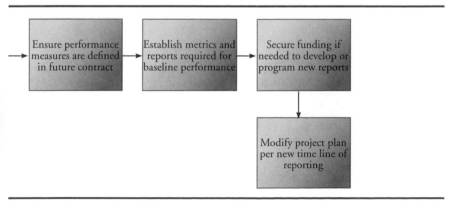

Question 5: Do you have an external rewards system in place to support desired outcomes?

Condition: Absolutely   Somewhat   Not Yet   Not Sure   Not Required

Observations: Caution.

Your feedback suggests that you do not believe it is necessary to have an external rewards system for this effort. Our experience indicates that your change project will not achieve desired outcomes if an external rewards system is not in place.

Recommendation: Ensure that you take steps to determine whether an internal rewards system is in place and/or required to support your change effort; namely:

- Immediately research whether an external rewards system is funded and approved by your key stakeholders and Finance
- Immediately research the consistency and objectivity of the external rewards system
- Immediately research whether the external rewards system is based upon the desired outcomes tied to SMART goals and objectives

Actions: An approach, as shown below in flow-charted form, will allow you to address whether an external rewards system should be in place and, as may be appropriate, to develop and gain approval for this system with key functions and stakeholders.

A SWOT Analysis Tool allows business executives to assess their current organization or organizational plan from a viewpoint that considers organizational strengths, weaknesses, opportunities and threats.

Typically these SWOT analyses are accomplished during an annual business planning cycle, however, they could just as easily be carried out as needed for Executive Management. A SWOT analysis would be useful in understanding the value of having an external provider rewards system in place to help achieve your goals and objectives.

The Risk Assessment Tool is designed to create a methodical approach to mitigating risks that are identified within areas of a project, a proposal a

Figure 6-5 Question 5 Action plan

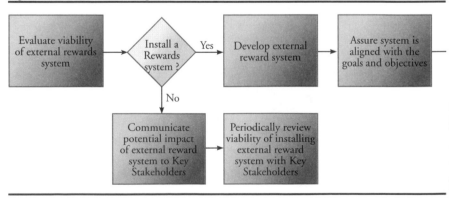

business marketplace, or anywhere risk is prevalent. The Risk Assessment Tool can use information derived from SWOT Tool or can be used as a stand-alone risk assessment vehicle. Basically, the Risk Assessment Tool provides a means for identification of inherent risks to the business; assessment of the potential impacts on the business if those risks were to manifest themselves in the business model; and, development and assignment of actions to mitigate the risks to prevent impairment of the business in meeting customer expectations.

ASSESSMENT IMPACT AND CHANGE IMPLEMENTATION

Depending upon the project you are leading, there may be other outcomes in the area of incentive that must be assessed. The opportunity to add additional questions, which provide more insight and involve more preparation, is always an available option. Unique projects may require focused attention in the area of government approval or support, corporate policy changes, legal ramifications, or financial considerations to name a few. Areas like these may require their own questions that, in turn, must be assessed to ensure a successful change effort.

Once you have completed your assessment in the **Driving Complex Change®** element of incentive, you will understand your strengths as well as those areas that need increased focus in order to successfully effect change. Expected outcomes include:

- Understanding if defined goals and objectives are in place
- Understanding if goals and objectives are measurable and achievable (SMART)
- Identifying if an internal rewards system is in place and/or required
- Understanding the capabilities of the current measurement and reporting process
- Identifying if an external rewards system is in place and/or required

By ensuring that key aspects of incentive are in place, you have enabled a key element which supports successful implementation of complex change within your organization/company.

Resource Element - Focus and Analysis

Key topics covered in this chapter ....

- Resource Element
  - Current State Assessment
  - Future State Development

- Assessment Impact and Change Implementation

"Alone we can do so little, together we can do so much."
- Helen Keller

INTRODUCTION

We have defined **Driving Complex Change®** methodology in terms of change management success and the related application of a practical assessment framework focused on the underlying elements – direction, ability, incentive resources, structure and action – and self-applied diagnostics and actionable feedback.   We have reviewed the standardized, controlled approach and utilized a series of questions in the areas of direction, ability and incentive to guide the user through a step-by-step analysis.   These questions assess the current state, design the future state, and provide controlled practices to close gaps and reduce risks.   We will now move through another set of questions in the element of resources.

> "Alignment is a time honored challenge.   But for several reasons, it is today taking on greater urgency.   First, project proliferation is consuming increasing levels of precious resources, without necessarily producing commensurate business results. Second, today's earnings-driven economy demands greater project utility to recapture investor confidence and unlock hidden shareholder value.   And finally, the evolving marketplace and its increasing unpredictability compounds the challenge of meeting current objectives while also preparing for the future."
>
> – Cathleen Benko, and F. Warren McFarlan[1]

RESOURCES - ASSESSMENT, OBSERVATIONS, RECOMMENDATIONS AND ACTIONS

Earlier we defined resources as "the appropriate allocation of human, financial and technical capabilities required to complete the appropriate activities needed for a successful outcome".   We will now identify the key assessment questions that are a part of this element and why they are important.   With that in place, we will then review each question against a selected condition in order to address the observations, recommendations and actions (ORA) presented.   Each question will also include a listing of support tools and processes that can be applied to any exposures.

CURRENT STATE ASSESSMENT – KEY QUESTIONS AND ASSESSMENTS

We have developed the following set of pertinent questions that focus on ensuring that this element – resources – is prepared to support a major change effort:

Have you established a plan detailing all required resources?

A *resource plan* outlines the support needed for your change project to be successful. This plan identifies personnel requirements, capital equipment and expenses required to successfully complete your project.   It is critical to the success of any change project that an accurate resource plan be established in order for the company to clearly understand what is required to successfully change a function.   Typical resource plans call for more initial cost during the start-up phase with the cost savings coming back to the company after the changed function has matured.

Has your resource plan been approved by the Executive Stakeholders and is it being funded in the current budget?

Executive Stakeholder approval is very important to the success of your change project.   This level of approval ensures that the resources necessary to support your change project will be made available to you when needed.   Budget approval is also critical at the beginning of any change project because costs are typically greatest during these early implementation stages with planned gains related to

---

[1] Connecting the Dots - Aligning Projects with Objectives in Unpredictable Times (Harvard Business School Publishing, 2003).

productivity improvements and cost reductions realized after project completion. Without budget approval, you will likely encounter difficulty acquiring required resources as the project progresses. This will cause delays to the schedule as you seek financial approval outside of the normal budgeting process.

Do you have the tools and skills to manage the resources for this effort?

Managing the multiple resources required to successfully complete a change project requires a highly experienced project management skill set with an in-depth understanding of change management requirements. There are many different tools that can be employed to help manage this complexity. Typical change projects require coordination between your Operations, Human Resources, Finance, Legal and Information Technology organizations, among others. The timely completion of deliverables is necessary for the successful completion of any change project.

Do you have a mechanism in place for communication and status reporting activities?

Having standardized methodologies in place that ensure timely communication and status reporting to key stakeholders, cross-functional organizations and your project team is a critical component to the success of your change project. Poor communication and unclear statuses are main contributors to not meeting project timelines and/or goals. Your mechanism for communication and status reporting must be effective and encompass the right stakeholder audience. Key components to an effective communication mechanism include face-to-face meetings, status reports, dashboards, and financials; and, they need to involve appropriate elements of the stakeholder audience at the right intervals. It is critical to change management to have a good communication process in place.

Are the resources available for the timeframe that you require?

As you move forward through the different stages of your change project, resources will be required at different intervals. This can be support from different functions such as Operations/Business, Finance, Legal, Human Resources, and Information Technology, or it could be financial support in the area of hardware, software, equipment or consultants. Coordination of the headcount resources is always a critical factor because these functions have many commitments and you need to ensure that your project has the correct priority within their organizations. Financial approvals for expenses during different quarters should already be approved upfront, otherwise delays could occur.

FUTURE STATE DEVELOPMENT – OBSERVATIONS, RECOMMENDATIONS AND ACTIONS

We will now focus on the element of resources as it pertains to the scenario we established in Chapter 4. As a reminder, the following is a brief outline of our scenario, with some additional focus on this element.

Scenario Example

"You have been designated as the Program Manager of a major restructuring effort within your company (ABC). ABC has just completed the acquisition of another company."

"This effort has many stakeholders and will require the integration of the new company (XYZ) into the current organization within ABC."

"This project will include outsourcing specific functions not considered core competencies; and, core competencies will need to be agreed upon and plans for disinvestment will need to be developed."

"Existing business practices are partially documented and distributed, yet there is much risk in the undocumented practices and in the readiness to move them to an outsourced provider. The processes will need to be institutionalized and measured to determine if the restructuring objectives and goals are being achieved."

"Your project team has developed a detailed resource plan. You have strong support from your Executive Stakeholders; however, all budget approvals have not yet been received. At this time there is no one on the project team with Project Management and Change Management experience and skills, but you are looking to transfer over an experienced Project Manager from another organization."

"You are unaware of any established communication or reporting process for the project. This has been a low priority item that you have not addressed."

"Determining if resources are available for your project is not required because this project is a high priority and everyone should be supporting it."

There are questions in the element of resources that you need to ask as well as answers to evaluate to ensure that your team can be successful. The following is a look at five questions that should be asked in this scenario, the condition that exists in relation to each question and observations, recommendations and actions, which should be followed.

Question 1 Have you established a plan detailing all required resources?

Condition:	Absolutely	Somewhat	Not Yet	Not Sure	Not Required

Observations: Excellent!

Your feedback suggests that you have taken the necessary steps to develop a resource plan that identifies what headcount will have to be provided to support the upcoming change; what capital equipment must be ordered for the project; and, what expenses are required to successfully complete your project.

It is critical to the success of any change project that an accurate resource plan be established, and that the company clearly understand what is required to successfully change a function. Typical resource plans call for more initial cost during the start-up phase with the cost savings coming back to the company after the changed function has matured.

Recommendation: Your follow-up should stress building and maintaining credibility for your resource plan through adherence to these critical elements:

- Ensure that the resource plan is agreed to by the key stakeholders and project team members.
- Ensure that your Finance representative agrees with and supports your resource plan.
- Communicate the resource plan to Human Resources, Legal, Information Technology and the Operations/Business management team to ensure that everyone supports the resource plan.

Actions: An approach, as shown below in flow-charted form, will allow you to review and gain support for your resource plan with key stakeholders.

Support Tools: Resource Plans help to define the entire resources required to implement change effectively. There are many areas where resources are required to successfully change a function or process.

From a personnel perspective, no area should be overlooked. Personnel listed within a resource plan could include Subject Matter Experts, Key Stakeholders, Executive Stakeholders and representatives from Information Technology, Finance, Human Resources and Legal. There are many other key areas that need to be covered when it comes to a successful resource plan. This can include budget, facilities, equipment, software, hardware, and external support.

You have to understand what resources you need to be successful and, in addition, you have to gain approval for these resources; to lobby for the right

Figure 7-1 Question 1 Action plan

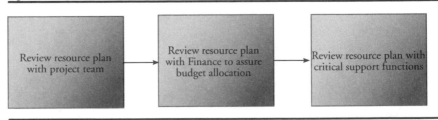

people to be engaged; and to be able to map out these resources; ensuring that they will be available when you need them. A comprehensive resource plan lists what resources are needed to be successful, when they are needed, and their current status.

Question 2 Has your resource plan been approved by the Executive Stakeholders and is it being funded in the current budget?

Condition: Absolutely   Somewhat   Not Yet   Not Sure   Not Required

Observations: Based upon your feedback this could be an area of exposure. Executive Stakeholder approval is typically very important to the success your change project. This level of approval ensures that the resources necessary to support your change project will be made available to you when needed.

Budget approval is also critical at the beginning of any change project because costs are typically greatest during these early implementation stages with planned gains related to productivity improvements and cost reductions realized after project completion. Without budget approval, you will likely encounter difficulty acquiring required resources as the project progresses. This will cause delays to the schedule as you seek financial approval outside of the normal budgeting process.

When either of these two items is missing, you may still be all right if the scope of the change project is small; or if you are in a small to mid-size company and have your CEO's approval/mandate.

Recommendation: With these observations in mind, taking the following steps to ensure that key functions and stakeholders are on board and aligned with your resource plan and funding requirements are critical to project success:

- Validate the current support for your project; the current budget allocation; the scope of your project; and typical approvals necessary within your company to secure resources for a project. If you determine there is an exposure, take actions to fill the gaps.
- Ensure your Executive Stakeholders are on board to ensure support and minimize roadblocks.
- Ensure that funding is available for your project, either through your company's budget process, or through an Executive Management mandate that supports your project.
- Ensure that your Finance representative on the team agrees that you have the company's financial support.

Actions: An iterative approach, as shown below in flow-charted form, will allow you to keep your key functions and stakeholders engaged and aligned with your resource plan and ongoing levels of support.

Support Tools: Return On Investment (ROI) is a return ratio that compares the net benefits of a project verses its total costs. ROI is a measurement of operating performance

Figure 7-2 Question 2 Action plan

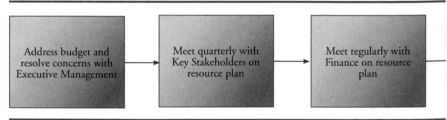

and efficiency in utilizing assets by a company. With this measure in place, you can determine the size of the benefit to the company; how long it will take for the benefits to be realized; and where the benefits will occur. Typically an ROI is required up front for major projects such as acquisitions in order to validate the benefits of the projects. Your Finance organization plays a large role in the development, approval and support of an ROI. Once completed, it should not be placed on a shelf and forgotten, but utilized as a reference to validate that the company is realizing the desired benefits.

Question 3 Do you have the tools and skills to manage the resources for this effort?

| Condition: | Absolutely | Somewhat | Not Yet | Not Sure | Not Required |

Observations: Your feedback suggests that you have not secured the skills or tools to manage the resources required to complete your change project. This could be a major exposure to your project due to the many challenges of managing and coordinating the multiple resources required to successfully complete your project.

Most large change projects are very complex and require a highly experienced project management skill set with an in-depth understanding of change management requirements. Adequate tools to keep track of the project resources, and to coordinate those resources are equally important. Typical change projects require coordination between your Operations team, Human Resources, Finance, Legal, and Information Technology, among others. The timing for completion of deliverables is basic to the successful completion of a change project. Without having either the skills available to manage the project resources or the tools to coordinate these resources, your project could miss planned completion times for specific milestones.

Recommendation: With any major change effort, project management skills to manage and coordinate project resources should be addressed early on and re-enforced periodically throughout the effort. This should include the following:

- Define the resources required to achieve success.
- Determine where gaps exist in either the skills or tools to manage the resources.
- Determine the best action to take in order to acquire the skills and tools required to manage the project resources.
- Ensure that you have key stakeholder approval and support for actions defined by your team to acquire the skills and tools required to manage the project resources.
- Ensure that you have the additional resource approval required to fill the skills and tools gap. This may require the transfer of internal headcount and/or an engagement with a consultant.
- Review your project milestones and time lines to account for the additional time required to fill the gaps in either skills or tools.

Actions: An approach, as shown below in flow-charted form, will allow you to define and justify project management skill and tool requirements with your key stakeholders and implement changes within your project and support teams.

Figure 7-3 Question 3 Action plan

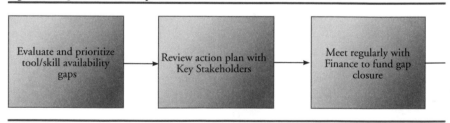

| Evaluate and prioritize tool/skill availability gaps | → | Review action plan with Key Stakeholders | → | Meet regularly with Finance to fund gap closure |

Support Tools   A *Project Management Tool* consolidates all the actionable records (those with delivery dates) into one centralized area. This allows for a common monitoring point as well as a single area for reporting of actionable records. The actionable records within a Project Management Tool are organized by date and by status of the deliverable. Typically these tools use an easy-to-view stoplight configuration, such as Red being for overdue records, Yellow being within 7 days of due date, and Green for on track records. This tri-colored graphical summary makes it easier to determine the status of projects and to quickly identify the owner of those deliverables.

A *Communication Planning Tool* is designed to assist management with a structured means to organize essential communications tasks in support of broad scale change in the business environment. The tool allows the user to identify various types of communications; the audience of those communications; who owns developing and delivering the communications; the appropriate method of delivery; and the frequency of delivery. This tool also captures the expected outcome and due dates for the messaging.

A *Communication Planning Tool* also enables a methodical approach to communications such that the author can plan, and deliver, the communications with an increased probability of a successful outcome. An established approach enables confidence in communications, which will improve the likelihood that the targeted audiences will receive the required information in the intended timeframes to improve understanding, alignment, and adoption of the planned transformation. Communication is the cornerstone of a successful business transformation management plan, and a *Communication Planning Tool* enables greater degrees of awareness, planning and thought into this critical area.

| Update project plan as required | → | Meet and report regularly the status of issues with Key Stakeholders | → | Meet and report regularly the status of issues with Project/Support teams |

Question 4 Do you have a mechanism in place for communication and status reporting activities?

Condition: Absolutely   Somewhat   Not Yet   Not Sure   Not Required

Observations: Your feedback suggests that you are unsure whether you have a mechanism to communicate effectively on your change project. This could be an exposure area.

If you do not have an effective communication mechanism, then your key stakeholders, cross-functional supporters, project team members and an external Provider may not receive communications and statuses as required. This would make it appear that your project has fallen into a "black hole". Executive Management will be concerned that the project is off course, when, in fact, it could be doing very well. There may be confusion among the team members, cross-functional teams and an external Provider, causing delays in the project plan. It is extremely important that you ensure that you have an effective communication mechanism in place, regardless of the size of the change project.

Key components to an effective communication mechanism include face-to-face meetings, status reports, dashboards, and financials; and they need to involve appropriate elements of the stakeholder audience at the right intervals. If you do not have the skills or tools to improve your communication mechanism, then you should look external to your organization, either inside or outside your company, for support. Timely and effective communications aid a change project and contribute to its success.

Recommendation: Review whether you have an effective communication mechanism in place.

> ° If yes;

>> - Ensure that you have an effective communication plan in place; and,
>> - Ensure that key stakeholders, team members, and cross-functional team members are included.

Figure 7-4 Question 4 Action plan

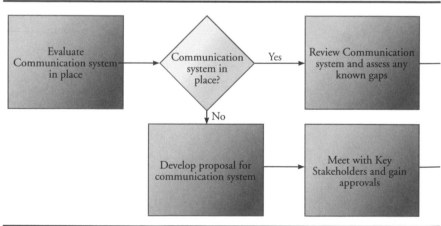

○ If no;

- Determine if you have the skills, knowledge and tools within your organization to develop and implement an effective communication mechanism;
- Secure the resources required, both internal and external to your company, to fill the gaps;
- Gain approvals from your key stakeholders and Finance; and then,
- Update your project plan milestones and time line.

Actions: A framework, as shown below in flow-charted form, will allow you to not only evaluate whether you have a communication mechanism in place, but also to develop and gain approval for one with key functions and stakeholders if you do not.

Support Tools: A *Communication Planning Tool* is designed to assist management with a structured means to organize essential communications tasks in support of broad scale change in the business environment. The tool allows the user to identify various types of communications; the audience of those communications; who owns developing and delivering the communications; the appropriate method of delivery; and the frequency of delivery. This tool also captures the expected outcome and due dates for the messaging.

A *Communication Planning Tool* also enables a methodical approach to communications such that the author can plan, and deliver, the communications with an increased probability of a successful outcome. An established approach enables confidence in communications, which will improve the likelihood that the targeted audiences will receive the required information in the intended timeframes to improve understanding, alignment, and adoption of the planned transformation. Communication is the cornerstone of a successful business transformation management plan, and a *Communication Planning Tool* allows greater degrees of awareness, planning and thought into this critical area.

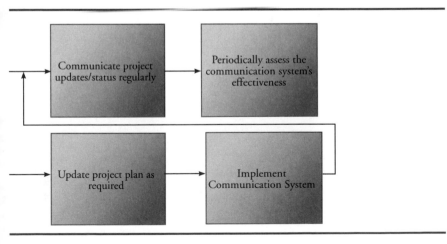

Question 5 Are the resources available for the timeframe that you require?

Condition:	Absolutely	Somewhat	Not Yet	Not Sure	**Not Required**

Observations: Caution.

Your feedback suggests that resource availability and commitment is not required for your change project. There are few occasions where this could be acceptable. If, for example, you are a small to mid-size company and you have a mandate from your CEO, then resource availability may be provided as needed; or perhaps an external company that specializes in your project's scope of change is managing the project.

If you are not planning on utilizing your current processes or tools, then gaining resource commitment internally to your company may not be a major requirement. Our experience tells us that regardless of the scope of the change project, there are always some internal resource requirements, which should be secured prior to moving forward. We suggest that you take a closer look to ensure that this is not the case.

Recommendation: Your follow-up should stress building and maintaining credibility for your resource and project plans and ongoing support commitments through adherence to these critical steps; namely:

- Review your resource plan. Understand whether there are any requirements for internal support of these resources. If so, determine if there are gaps and non-commitment, which could derail your change project.
- Develop an action plan to address any gaps. This could include securing internal and external resources.
- Periodically review the resource plan with your key stakeholders, ensuring they still support the plan and commit the required resources.
- Update your project plan as needed.

Figure 7-5 Question 5 Action plan

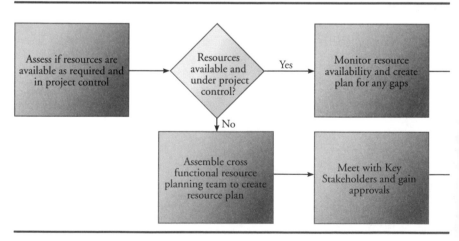

Actions: A framework, as shown below in flow-charted form, will allow you to not only review and affirm that ongoing resource availability and commitments are in place, but also to develop and gain approval for a new or revised resource plan with key functions and stakeholders if they are not.

Support Tools: Resource Plans help to define the entire resources required to implement change effectively. There are many areas where resources are required to successfully change a function or process.

From a personnel perspective, no one area should be overlooked. Personnel listed within a resource plan could include Subject Matter Experts, Key Stakeholders, Executive Stakeholders and representatives from Information Technology, Finance, Human Resources and Legal. There are many other key areas that need to be covered when it comes to a successful resource plan. This can include budget, facilities, equipment, software, hardware, and external support.

You have to understand what resources you need to be successful, and in addition, you have to gain approval for these resources; to lobby for the right people to be engaged; and to be able to map out these resources; ensuring that they will be available when you need them. A comprehensive resource plan lists what resources are needed to be successful, when they are needed, and their current status.

An *Action Plan* is a short-term plan, which highlights an area of concern, action items which will address the area of concern, time line, and resource requirements. This plan is presented to Management, and is then used to track the actions necessary to eliminate the area of concern to closure. These planned actions may also be called a *Corrective Action Plan*, which is generally used to define a process to eliminate the cause of a detected nonconformity, and in some instances, multiple non conformities.

Corrective action is taken to prevent recurrence. Correction relates to containment whereas corrective action relates to the root cause. A corrective

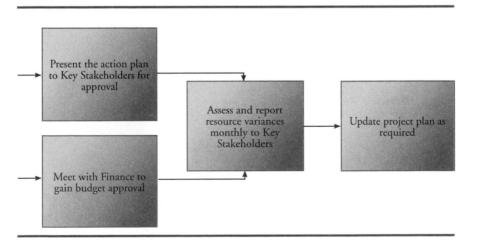

action plan should include a short-term fix to ensure that the current process is prevented from further risk or exposure. Additionally, a long-term cost/risk weighted action, based upon an understanding of the product or process involved, should be taken to prevent the problem from reoccurring.

The corrective action plan can also address inadequate "conditions", which may produce a nonconformance. In this application, the corrective action plan should include root cause analysis and process change directions to correct the nonconformity, and possibly, data indicating the current and future potential exposure to the nonconformity as well.

ASSESSMENT IMPACT AND CHANGE IMPLEMENTATION

Depending upon the project you are leading, there may be other outcomes in the area of resources that must be assessed. The opportunity to add additional questions, which provide more insight and greater preparation, is always an available option. Unique projects may require focused attention in the area of government approval or support, corporate policy changes, legal ramifications, or financial considerations to name a few. Areas like these may require their own questions that, in turn, must be assessed to ensure a successful change effort.

Once you've completed your assessment in the **Driving Complex Change®** element of resources, you will understand your strengths as well as those areas that need increased focus in order to successfully effect change. Expected outcomes include:

  * Identifying your resource requirements
  * Understanding if a resource plan is in place, approved and budgeted
  * Understanding if you have the tools and skills to manage the required resources
  * Identifying your communication methodology and plan
  * Understanding if the required resources are available when you need them

By ensuring that key aspects of resources are in place, you have enabled a key element which supports successful implementation of complex change within your organization or company.

Structure Element - Focus and Analysis

Key topics covered in this chapter ....

- Structure Element
  - Current State Assessment
  - Future State Development

- Assessment Impact and Change
  Implementation

"The best teams I've encountered have one important thing in common: their team structure and processes cover a full range of distinct competencies necessary for success."

- Jesse J. Garret

INTRODUCTION

We have defined **Driving Complex Change®** methodology in terms of change management success and the related application of a practical assessment framework focused on the underlying elements – direction, ability, incentive resources, structure and action – and self-applied diagnostics and actionable feedback.   We have reviewed the standardized, controlled approach and utilized a series of questions in the areas of direction, ability, incentive and resources to guide the user through a step-by-step analysis. These questions assess the current state, design the future state, and provide controlled practices to close gaps and reduce risks.   We will now move through another set of questions in the element of structure.

STRUCTURE - ASSESSMENT, OBSERVATIONS, RECOMMENDATIONS AND ACTIONS

Earlier we defined structure as "the elements of a company's business system and their relationship to the predictability of a successful program". We will now identify the key assessment questions that are a part of this element and why they are important. With that in place, we will then review each question against a selected condition in order to address the observations, recommendations and actions (ORA) presented. Each question will also include a listing of support tools and processes that can be applied to any exposures.

> "Although some entrepreneurs resist structure because they fear it will inhibit creativity, establishing an organizational structure with clearly delineated roles and responsibilities actually promotes creativity rather than stifling it."
>
> – Katherine Catin and Jana Mathews[1]

CURRENT STATE ASSESSMENT – KEY QUESTIONS AND ASSESSMENTS

We have developed the following set of pertinent questions that focus on ensuring that this element – structure – is prepared to support a major change effort:

Do you have a documented Quality Management System in place for all key processes and procedures?

A documented *Quality Management System* controls all processes and procedures in a predictable, sustainable and flexible way. Processes and procedures are revision controlled, documented, and auditable, and corrective action plans are implemented when gaps are found. Metrics and goals have been established to track performance; reporting is in place; and frequent communication is made to Executive Management. Utilizing documented processes and procedures enables consistent performance. An effective Quality Management System greatly increases the opportunity for a successful change project.

Do you have a Service Level Agreement with your internal service providers?

A *Service Level Agreement* (SLA) with an internal service provider, such as an Information Technology provider, means that you have established the support requirements necessary for a given function. Performance metrics are in place in order to measure the effectiveness of the internal service provider,

---

[1] Leading at the Speed of Growth, by Katherine Catin and Jana Mathews (Copyright 2001, Kauffman Center for Entrepreneurial Leadership, Ewing Marion Kauffman Foundation).

enabling the ability to provide feedback and establish corrective actions for needed improvements. It is important to understand the support requirements from internal service providers to any function that you plan to change. These support requirements will need to continue in the future, whether they are provided by the same internal service providers or by a new support structure that is put in place.

Do you have a thorough understanding of the processes that you are considering for change?

It is important to map out all of the processes being utilized by the function to be changed. This map should accurately reflect both the work being done today, as well as the processes being utilized consistently by the function's personnel. You are aware of all the interdependencies that exist; and understand the metrics being tracked and the delivery of the current performance measures; what support is being provided by internal service providers, and what systems are being used; and which personnel must be within scope for the outsourcing project to be successful. The processes must also be documented as part of the transfer of information necessary to support the changing project, and to ensure a smooth handoff to an external Provider if outsourcing.

Is today's process measured, goaled and rewarded based upon performance?

When a process is measured, goaled and rewarded on performance, it enables your project team to understand what is necessary to help the company be successful; that is, objective measurements ensure the performance of the process; goals set the target for performance; and rewarding performance reinforces the positive achievements that are accomplished. A gap in any one of these three steps can impact the performance of a team. Without measurement, you cannot track performance; without goals, you cannot set higher levels of achievement; and without rewarding performance, the team may lack incentive to achieve the goals.

Do you have a documented information flow for systems capture?

Documented information flow for systems capture means that you have mapped how the software applications interrelate, and how they support the function to be changed. This means that you understand the interdependencies of the systems being utilized, and how they support and rely on one another; what software applications are necessary to successfully support the function; and what reports and data that are needed to manage and take action.

Having the information flow documented, enables you to understand the system and software application dependencies that exist for the function being changed. This enables the project team to ensure that all system and software application requirements are in place or replaced as necessary. Without this in place, you risk the process failing due to one of these dependencies not being in place during the execution of the process.

FUTURE STATE DEVELOPMENT – OBSERVATIONS, RECOMMENDATIONS AND ACTIONS

We will now focus on the element of **structure** as it pertains to the scenario we established in Chapter 4. As a reminder, the following is a brief outline of our scenario, with additional focus on this element.

Scenario Example

"You have been designated as the Program Manager of a major restructuring effort within your company (ABC). ABC has just completed the acquisition of another company."

"This effort has many stakeholders and will require the integration of the new company (XYZ) into current organization within ABC."

"This project will include outsourcing specific functions not considered core competencies; and, core competencies will need to be agreed upon, and plans for disinvestment will need to be developed."

"Existing business practices are partially documented and distributed, yet there is much risk in the undocumented practices and the readiness to move them to an outsourced provider. The processes will need to be institutionalized and measured to determine if the objectives and goals are being achieved."

"Your company is ISO9001 certified, which is supported by a mature Quality Management System. There is one Service Level Agreement in place with Information Technology for the function being outsourced, however, there is nothing in place with Operations, which also provides support."

"Your team has not yet reviewed and assessed all of the processes that are utilized by the function. This means that you do not know how today's process is measured, goaled and rewarded. Given the basic nature of the function, your team does not believe that it is necessary to document the information flow for systems capture."

There are questions in the element of structure that you need to ask, as well as answers to evaluate to ensure that your team can be successful. The following is a look at five questions that should be asked in this scenario; the condition that exists in relation to each question; and observations, recommendations and actions, which should be followed.

Question 1 Do you have a documented Quality Management System in place for all key processes and procedures?

Condition: Absolutely   Somewhat   Not Yet   Not Sure   Not Required

Observations: Excellent.

Your feedback suggests that you have a methodology in place to manage all of your processes and procedures. This means that your processes and procedures are managed in a predictable, sustainable and flexible way. They are revision controlled, documented, auditable, followed, and corrective action plans are implemented when gaps are found. There are metrics and goals established to track performance; and reporting and frequent communication to Executive Management are in place. When documented processes and procedures are followed, it establishes consistent performance. This greatly increases the opportunity for a successful change project.

Recommendation: Your follow-up should stress building and maintaining credibility for the methodology in place that manages the processes and procedures involved in the change project.

- Ensure that the key processes and procedures that are utilized by the function are documented and up to date.
- Ensure that the audit process has been closely adhered to, and validates that the documented processes and procedures are accurate and being followed.
- Ensure that metrics, goals, reporting and communication are in place and tracked, and that you initiate actions when necessary.

Actions: An approach, as shown below in flow-charted form, will allow you audit the performance of the key processes and procedures and validate the accuracy of your Quality Management System.

Support Tools: An *Assessment Management Tool* enables your company to perform assessments and audits required to evaluate current conditions, to capture potential business exposures before they occur, and to monitor compliance to standards. This tool enables you to schedule the assessment; define the type of assessment being performed and identify who will perform the assessment; and then capture the findings of the assessment. Dependent upon the findings, Corrective Action Resolutions may be initiated to track the activities being performed to correct the findings.

Figure 8-1 Question 1 Action plan

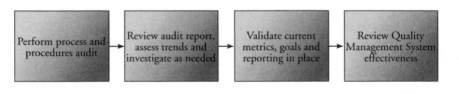

| Perform process and procedures audit | Review audit report, assess trends and investigate as needed | Validate current metrics, goals and reporting in place | Review Quality Management System effectiveness |

Question 2 Do you have a Service Level Agreement with your internal service providers?

Condition: Absolutely   Somewhat   Not Yet   Not Sure   Not Required

Observations: This could be an area of exposure to your change project. If your internal service providers, such as Information Technology, are going to be required to provide support, then a Service Level Agreement (SLA) should be established. If the intent is to take the entire function out of your company and not rely on any of your internal service providers for support, then this may not be a large exposure area. SLA's document the support to be provided and the associated metrics to be tracked. This agreement requires that the performance levels of the service provided be monitored so that you can ensure that the support meets the business need.

Recommendation: Determine whether any of your internal service providers are going to have to continue to provide support.

- If yes, you should ensure that you have SLAs in place for every internal service provider of the function. They need to be written with the understanding that the future support may be delivered externally.

- If no, you should ensure that the new support provider has the capabilities and scope to deliver all that has been required by the function's internal service providers.

Actions: A staged framework, as shown below in flow-charted form, will allow you to determine which of your internal service providers will be required to support the outsourced function and what new or existing SLAs must be in place.

Support Tools: Service Level Agreement (SLA) is a contract between two organizations or companies that specifies, usually in measurable terms, the services to be delivered. An SLA and a contract have much in common and are often confused with each other. There are some differences, however, that make it more appropriate, in some cases, to use a SLA rather than a contract. An SLA is a "proxy contract"; that is, a formal, negotiated agreement between two parties that takes the

Figure 8-2 Question 2 Action plan

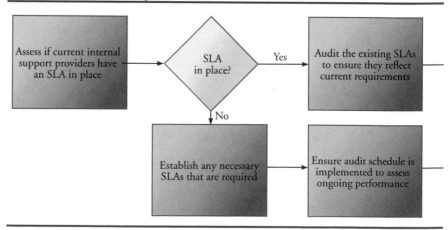

place of a formal contract, detailing the essential elements of services and quantifying the minimum level of service to be provided by the supplier, meets the business needs of the client. An SLA can be used as a stand-alone document or as a supplement to a contract. In either case, the agreed upon terms of the agreement are written in a formal document, which is signed by both parties. The document is amended regularly as a reflection of the customer's changing business needs and related changes in circumstances.

The three objectives that can be identified in a SLA are as follows:

- The recognition and statement of customer needs by providing a service statement. This statement can either stand on its own right, or be modified as a statement of customer needs with a schedule showing which services are selected from a larger list.
- Analyzes the processes of fulfilling that need by using statements of what is to be done. It does not say, however, how it is done, and thus is prescriptive and unrestrictive; that is, as it only states what is to be done and not how, the supplier can use different methods to do what has to be done; find improvements on the way to do it; and also have the freedom to develop it. The supplier's statement of needs is also provided by this second objective.
- Describes the means of measuring the performance in carrying out these processes. The levels of activity may also be defined, thus registering both the agreement of both parties and the relationship to their respective business needs.

The skills needed in making a SLA work include:

- **Negotiating** - the supplier and customer meet to discuss the service level that is to be provided.
- **Writing the agreement** - the agreed to terms from the negotiation written in a formal form.
- **Monitoring the performance** - the performance is constantly monitored to see if the SLA specifications have been achieved.
- **Issuing a SLA report** - meetings are held periodically to discuss customer

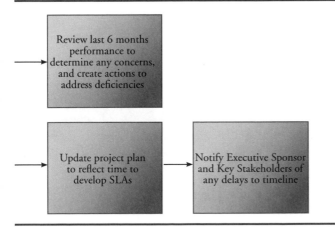

satisfaction. If necessary, the terms can be reviewed and the SLA revised.

The SLA, however, has no legal effect, as its purpose is to ensure that there is a common understanding of the required services to be provided. It is not intended to be a contract and only represents the goodwill of the parties signing it. If it fails, neither party can sue the other. Its use is appropriate for all in-house services that are departments within a company or where there is no legal contract.

Question 3 Do you have a thorough understanding of the processes that you are considering for change?

Condition: Absolutely   Somewhat   Not Yet   Not Sure   Not Required

Observations: If the scope of your project is to not utilize the processes currently being used, but rather to rely on the outsourced Provider's processes, then this may not be a large area of exposure.

By understanding the processes being utilized today by the function being changed, you are aware of all the interdependencies that exist; understand the metrics being tracked, the delivery of the current performance measures; what support is being provided by internal service providers; what systems are being used; and which personnel must be within scope for the change project to be successful.

> "In order to build the proper infrastructure, you need to ensure that:
>
> - The processes are written down and people understand them and acknowledge their value in streamlining the organization's work.
> - Employees throughout the organization know and use the same processes and are able to describe them to new people.
> - People know who in the organization is responsible for which processes.
> - The people who are responsible for a process provide training and support so employees know how to use the process and know where to turn when they need information or help."
>
> – Katherine Catin and Jana Mathews[2]

Figure 8-3 Question 3 Action plan

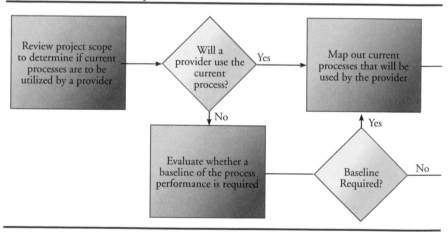

[2] Building the Awesome Organization – Six Essential Components that Drive Entrepreneurial Growth (Copyright 2002 Kauffman Center for Entrepreneurial Leadership, Ewing Marion Kauffman Foundation, Published by Hungry Minds Inc., *New York*).

If you expect the Provider to use any of these processes, you have potentially have a large exposure to your change project.

Recommendation: Determine whether a Provider is going to use any of the existing processes.

- If yes - all processes being utilized must be understood, documented and standardized.
    - ensure that the processes are documented with the understanding that the work is going to be performed by a Provider.
    - review the outsourcing project plan to ensure it reflects the above actions being taken.

- If no - understand that you will have no solid basis with which to compare the performance of the outsourced Provider; and, to do this accurately, you must baseline the current performance by understanding the current processes.

Actions: A staged approach, as shown below in flow-charted form, will allow you to understand which internal processes and related resources will be required to support the Provider and to track their delivery and performance.

Support Tools: The *Process Management Tool* is used to describe the current characteristics of a process, a managed sequence of steps, tasks, or activities that convert inputs to an output. By documenting the processes, a Provider will be able to understand how success was being achieved and then evaluate the following:

- How their core competencies can successfully integrate into the processes;
- How to simplify or improve the processes;
- How to achieve the same results and performance initially, and then increase results; and
- How to return financial benefit to the company.

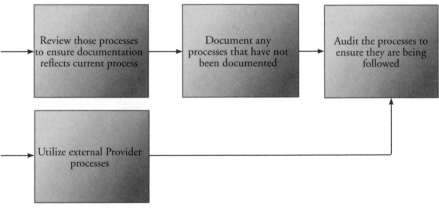

By utilizing the structured framework of the *Process Management Tool* you will describe the process steps, criteria or metrics used, desired improvements, and work instructions that are currently being used for each of the processes. These details will be the groundwork for analyzing potential providers for your Partnering project. The more detail provided, the more accurate your evaluation will be.

> "Nothing can grow in a self-sustaining way unless there are reinforcing processes underlying its growth. Therefore, thinking strategically about initiating, sustaining, and spreading fundamental management innovations over time requires appreciating the reinforcing processes that could cause such growth."
>
> – Peter Senge, Art Kleiner, Charlotte Roberts,
> Richard Ross, George Roth and Bryan Smith[3]

An *Assessment Management Tool* enables your company to perform assessments and audits as required to evaluate current conditions; to capture potential business exposures before they occur; and to monitor compliance to standards. This tool enables you to schedule the assessment; define the type of assessment being performed, identifies who will perform the assessment; and then captures the findings of the assessment. Dependent upon the findings, Corrective Action Resolutions may be initiated to track the activities being performed to correct the finding.

---

[3] The Dance of Change - The Challenges to Sustaining Momentum in Learning Organizations (Doubleday Publishers, 1999).

Question 4 Is today's process measured, goaled and rewarded based upon performance?

Condition: Absolutely   Somewhat   Not Yet   Not Sure   Not Required

Observations: Measurements ensure that the performance of the process is objective. Goals set the target for performance; and rewarding performance reinforces the positive achievements that are met. Your feedback suggests that this may or may not be occurring today.

It is important to understand how the process's performance is currently handled. If the process is measured, goaled and performance rewarded, then you have a great baseline in place; a methodology to set goals; and a performance reward process. If the process is not measured, goaled and performance rewarded, you will need to establish these steps. If the process is missing one or two of these steps, then you need to understand how this will be addressed.

> "Living systems have integrity. Their character depends on the whole. The same is true for organizations; to understand the most challenging managerial issues requires seeing the whole system that generates the issues."
>
> – Peter Senge [4]

Recommendation: Understand how the process is measured, goaled and if performance is rewarded; that is:

- If the process is measured, continue to track these metrics and ensure they are effective. If not measured, establish measures immediately.

- If the process is goaled, review the trends and determine if the goals are effective. If not goaled, establish goals with key stakeholders.

- If the process has a reward for performance methodology established, determine its effectiveness and modify if necessary. If the process does not have a reward for performance methodology in place, determine if necessary and if so, establish it.

Figure 8-4 Question 4 Action plan

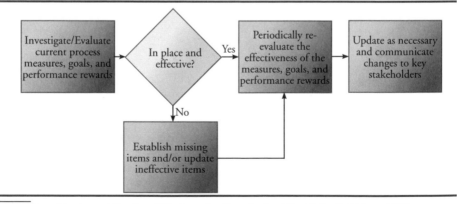

---

[4] The Fifth Discipline - The Art and Practice of The Learning Organization (Doubleday Publishers, 1990}.

Actions: A mapping approach, as shown below in flow-charted form, will allow you to understand how the process's performance is currently measured, rewarded and determine what steps need to be taken.

Support Tools: The *Process Management Tool* is used to describe the current characteristics of a process, a managed sequence of steps, tasks, or activities that convert inputs to an output. By documenting the processes, a Provider will be able to understand how success was being achieved and then evaluate the following:

- How their core competencies can successfully integrate into the processes.
- How to simplify or improve the processes.
- How to achieve the same results and performance initially, and then increase results.
- How to return financial benefit to the company.

By utilizing the structured framework of the Process Management Tool you will describe the process steps, criteria or metrics used, desired improvements, and work instructions that are currently being used for each of the processes. These details will be the groundwork for analyzing potential providers for your outsourcing project. The more detail provided, the more accurate your evaluation will be.

Question 5 Do you have a documented information flow for systems capture?

Condition: Absolutely   Somewhat   Not Yet   Not Sure | Not Required |

Observations: Your feedback indicates that you are not planning on using the current systems and software applications that are utilized by the function being changed. It is critical that you understand the new support structure's capabilities from a system and Software Application standpoint to ensure that they can meet your business requirements. This will be more difficult without the current information flow documented to guide you when comparing capabilities to the process requirements.

Recommendation: It is important that risks are mitigated if you are not requiring a documented information flow for the systems utilized within the process to be changed.
* Ensure the scoring for the new support structure's systems and software capabilities is weighted correctly given the exposure this area represents to the change project.
* Ensure that several super-users (personnel who understand the systems and software application requirements in-depth) evaluate the new support structure's capabilities in this area.
* Review the project plan time line and milestones to see if added steps need to be put in place to thoroughly test the systems and software application functionality before having the new support structure deliver the changed process.

Actions: Detailed steps, as shown below in flow-charted form, will provide a framework for reviewing the current state of information flow capture and the next steps that should be taken.

Figure 8-5 Question 5 Action plan

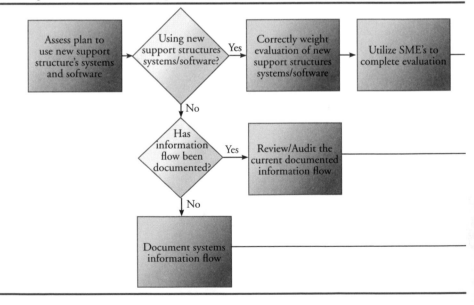

Support Tools: A Systems Map captures all of the systems and software applications that are used by a function. Typically every function uses at least one, if not many, software applications which are tied into the company's financial reporting, and management systems. When changing a function, the ties to these systems must be reassessed. It is critical that the your Information Technology department is engaged early, and is properly resourced to support the effort required to take the function external to the company. It is common to find that several interfaces or User Developed Applications, which are not documented, support the current function. A system mapping effort should also be completed prior to changing a process or function to fully understand the scope of the Information Technology activity involved.

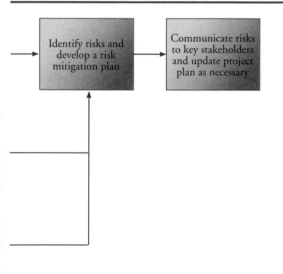

ASSESSMENT IMPACT AND CHANGE IMPLEMENTATION

Depending upon the project you are leading, there may be other outcomes in the area of structure that must be assessed. The opportunity to add additional questions, which provide more insight and involve more preparation, is always an available option. Unique projects may require focused attention in the area of government approval or support, corporate policy changes, legal ramifications, or financial considerations to name a few. Areas like these may require their own questions that, in turn, must be assessed to ensure a successful change effort.

Once you've completed your assessment in the **Driving Complex Change®** element of structure, you will understand your strengths as well as those areas that need an increased focus in order to successfully effect change. Expected outcomes include:

- Understanding if a Quality Management System is in place
- Identifying existing internal Service Level Agreements
- Identifying the processes being considered for change
- Understanding if these processes are measured, goaled and rewarded on performance
- Understanding if a Systems Map is in place

By ensuring that key aspects of structure are in place, you have enabled a key element which supports successful implementation of complex change within your organization or company.

Action Element - Focus and Analysis

Key topics covered in this chapter ....

- Action Element
    - ◼ Current State Assessment
    - ◼ Future State Development
- Assessment Impact and Change Implementation

"The most difficult thing is the decision to act, the rest is merely tenacity. The fears are paper tigers. You can do anything you decide to do."

- Robyn Davidson

INTRODUCTION

We have defined **Driving Complex Change®** methodology in terms of change management success and the related application of a practical assessment framework focused on the underlying elements – direction, ability, incentive resources, structure and action – and self-applied diagnostics and actionable feedback. We have reviewed the standardized, controlled approach and utilized a series of questions in the areas of direction, ability, incentive, resources and structure to guide the user through a step-by-step analysis. These questions assess the current state, design the future state, and provide controlled practices to close gaps and mitigate risks. We will now move through another set of questions in the element of action.

ACTION - ASSESSMENT, OBSERVATIONS, RECOMMENDATIONS AND ACTIONS

Earlier we defined *action* as *"the overall depth and breadth of the project plan"*. We will now identify the key assessment questions that are a part of this element and why they are important. With that in place, we will then review each question against a selected condition in order to address the observations, recommendations and actions (ORA) presented. Each question will also include a listing of support tools and processes that can be applied to any exposures.

> "Never mistake motion for action."
>
> – Ernest Hemingway[1]

CURRENT STATE ASSESSMENT – KEY QUESTIONS AND ASSESSMENTS

We have developed the following set of pertinent questions that focus on ensuring that this element – *action* – is prepared to support a major change effort:

Is your project approved, funded, and resourced?

Project approval ensures that you have Executive Management approval to proceed with your change project. This informs your organization and the cross-functional support teams that your project is a priority for the company. This provides a level of importance and leverage to your project team. Securing project funding validates that the company understands and supports the costs associated with completing your change project. Having the required resources allocated displays the company's commitment to the success of your change project. It is extremely important that you secure approval for the process as well as the financial support and resources necessary to effect change successfully.

Do you have a communication strategy to manage stakeholder expectations?

A successful communication strategy will ensure that your stakeholders are kept up to date on your project. Components of this strategy include the owner and sponsor of the strategy; stakeholders and stakeholder functional areas and expectations; required communication content, venues utilized, and timing; and, responsible communicator. By mapping out your communication strategy at the beginning of your change project, you will be able to develop a comprehensive and effective communication plan, which will support your project.

---

[1] In To Your Success, compiled by Dan Zadra and designed by Kobi Yamada and StevePotter (Copyright 1997 by Compendium, Inc., Published by Compendium, Inc. Publishing and Communications, Edmonds, WA).

Do you have a process to manage shortfalls, issues, and escalations?

Managing *shortfalls* indicates that your project has the checks and balances in place to know when you are missing a deadline, a deliverable may not be as complete as required, or any thing else, which causes your project to fall short of plan. There are usually many causes, and your process must find the root cause for the shortfall, correct the cause, and put the controls in place to ensure it doesn't happen again. Managing issues indicates that you have a process to acknowledge an issue, track the issue, and develop and implement a solution for the issue. Managing escalations means that, as these are received, you have a process to acknowledge receipt, track the escalation, direct it to the owner, implement the corrective action, notify the initiator, and close the escalation. By tracking issues and escalations, you will be able to recognize any trends that may be developing that require a more in-depth solution.

> "You can either take action, or you can hang back and hope for a miracle. Miracles are great, but they are so unpredictable."
>
> – Peter Drucker[2]

Do you have the program management skills and resources to deliver this effort?

The program management skills that are required to manage a change project are very complex and mature. They require handling of multiple milestones being supported by internal and external resources. Constant communication, milestone checks and statuses must be coordinated and evaluated. Informing the key stakeholders on a regular basis is extremely important. Managing the cost envelope and tracking the Return On Investment (ROI) are also important. The program management resources typically fall into two categories, personnel and tools. It is important that the program management personnel have the correct skills and experience to support your change project. It is also important that the right program management tools are available and utilized. There are many tools in this area that will work sufficiently. The best tools are the ones that can be accessed by multiple resources so that updates are made on a timely basis.

Do you thoroughly understand the enabler processes required to obtain and utilize the project resources?

It is important to realize that each subcomponent of your project could require a different process to be completed. Your project requires Executive Management and stakeholder approval. This would include a budget, which must be supported through the Finance team and planned into your company's *Medium Range Plan* (MRP). Capital equipment typically follows its own approval process that also involves Finance support and MRP inclusion. Internal headcount resources will need to be allocated, which will require management approval, and may possibly include training to support the coverage model. External headcount resources require the support of Finance as well as a headcount requisition or consultant contract, which must be approved and budgeted. Information Technology will need to determine what additional resources they will need to support your project, while maintaining current development and support programs. Each approval or planning session has its own process schedule which takes time to complete. You need to understand these requirements, schedules, and time requirements to ensure that your project plan accurately reflects what is required to complete your project.

FUTURE STATE DEVELOPMENT – OBSERVATIONS, RECOMMENDATIONS AND ACTIONS

We will now focus on the element of action as it pertains to the scenario we established in Chapter 4. As a reminder, the following is a brief outline of our scenario, with additional focus on this element.

---

[2] In To Your Success, compiled by Dan Zadra and designed by Kobi Yamada and StevePotter (Copyright 1997 by Compendium, Inc.,Published by Compendium, Inc. Publishing and Communications, Edmonds, WA).

Scenario Example

"You have been designated as the Program Manager of a major restructuring effort within your company (ABC). ABC has just completed the acquisition of another company."

"This effort has many stakeholders and will require the integration of the new company (XYZ) into current organization within ABC."

"This project will include outsourcing specific functions not considered core competencies; and, core competencies will need to be agreed upon, and plans for disinvestment will need to be developed."

"Existing business practices are partially documented and distributed, yet there is much risk in the undocumented practices and the readiness to move them to an outsourced provider. The processes will need to be institutionalized and measured to determine if the objectives and goals are being achieved."

"Your project has been approved, funding has been allocated, and resources have been committed. Your project team has started to draft a communication strategy, which will manage the broad base of project's stakeholders. To date, your project has not defined a process to manage shortfalls, issues or escalations. There is a targeted future date to develop this process."

"You are unsure if the program management skills and resources are available to support your project. Your project team believes that there is no requirement to understand any enabler processes to obtain resources required by the project."

There are questions in the element of *action* that you need to ask as well as answers to evaluate to ensure that your team can be successful. The following is a look at five questions that should be asked in this scenario, the condition that exists in relation to each question and *observations*, *recommendations* and *actions*, which should be followed.

"In successful change efforts, empowered people create short-term wins - victories that nourish faith in the change effort, emotionally reward the hard workers, keep the critics at bay, and build momentum."

- John P. Kotter and Dan S. Cohen[3]

---

[3] The Heart of Change (Copyright 2002 John P.Kotter and Deloitte Consulting LLC, Harvard Business School Publishing)

Question 1 Is your project approved, funded, and resourced?

Condition:	Absolutely	Somewhat	Not Yet	Not Sure	Not Required

Observations: Excellent. Your feedback suggests that your project is approved, funded and resourced. This means that you have gained project approval from your Executive Stakeholders and cross-functional management teams, and that they have approved and secured budget allocation for project costs, and have committed to make available the resources required when necessary to complete your change project. With this type of alignment and support, your change project is on the right track.

Recommendation: With these observations in mind, maintaining key stakeholder commitments for project resources is critical to success:

- Ensure that you continue to update your key stakeholders to maintain their level of involvement to ensure that they are engaged.
- Ensure that the signoff process is closely followed.
- Ensure that costs are closely tracked and mapped against planned spending.
- Ensure that your resource plan is periodically reviewed with key stakeholders.

Actions: An iterative communications approach, as shown below in flow-charted form, will allow you to keep your key stakeholders informed of your project status and aligned with project resource commitments.

Support Tools: A *Communication Planning Tool* is designed to assist management with a structured means to organize essential communication tasks in support of broad scale change in the business environment. The tool allows the user to identify various types of communications; the audience of those communications; who owns developing and delivering the communications; the appropriate method of delivery; and, the frequency of delivery. This tool also captures the expected outcome and due dates for the messaging.

A *Communication Planning Tool* also enables a methodical approach to communications such that the author can plan, and deliver, the communications with an increased probability of a successful outcome. An established approach enables confidence in communications, which will improve the likelihood that the targeted audiences will receive the required information in the intended timeframes to improve understanding, alignment, and adoption of the planned transformation. Communication is the cornerstone of a successful business transformation management plan, and a *Communication Planning Tool* allows greater degrees of awareness, planning and thought into this critical area.

Figure 9-1 Question 1 Action plan

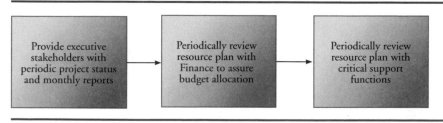

Question 2 Do you have a communication strategy to manage stakeholder expectations?

| Condition: | Absolutely | Somewhat | Not Yet | Not Sure | Not Required |

Observations: Your feedback suggests that your communication strategy is not fully developed to manage stakeholder expectations. This could be an area of exposure. It is extremely important that you ensure that you have established an effective communication strategy and communication plan that effectively manages stakeholder expectations. Key Stakeholders' understanding and commitment to the desired outcome, priorities, scope, and time lines are critical to any successful change project.

A successful communication strategy will ensure that your stakeholders are kept up to date on your project. Components to this strategy include the owner and sponsor of the strategy; stakeholders and stakeholder functional areas and expectations; required communication content, venues utilized, timing; and, identified communicator. By mapping out your communication strategy at the beginning of your change project, you will be able to develop a comprehensive and effective communication plan, which will support your project.

A key output of this communication strategy will be the development of a supporting communication plan. Components of this plan include the owner and sponsor of the plan; what you want to communicate and to whom and when; what venue is used to communicate; and, who is responsible to communicate.

Recommendation: Your follow-up should stress building and maintaining credibility for your communication strategy and supporting communication plan to meet and manage stakeholder understanding of project plans and statuses: namely:

- Ensure that you have a communication strategy in place for the key stakeholders to ensure their commitment to the change plan.
- Ensure that the communication strategy reflects an understanding of the stakeholders' realistic expectations, project scope and desired outcomes as well as stakeholder time lines for a successful change project.
- Ensure that you have a communication plan that supports your communication strategy.
- Ensure that owners are established within the communication plan and that they communicate per the plan.
- Ensure that the desired outcome, changes in priorities, project scope, and project time lines within the communication plan are aligned with the owners' expectations.

Figure 9-2 Question 2 Action plan

Actions: Steps, as shown below in flow-charted form, allow you to develop and maintain a credible communication strategy to meet key stakeholder expectations.

Support Tools: A *Communication Planning Tool* is designed to assist management with a structured means to organize essential communications tasks in support of broad scale change in the business environment. The tool allows the user to identify various types of communications; the audience of those communications; who owns developing and delivering the communications; the appropriate method of delivery; and, the frequency of delivery. This tool also captures the expected outcome and due dates for the messaging.

A *Communication Planning Tool* also enables a methodical approach to communications such that the author can plan, and deliver, the communications with an increased probability of a successful outcome. An established approach enables confidence in communications, which will improve the likelihood that the targeted audiences will receive the required information in the intended timeframes to improve understanding, alignment, and adoption of the planned transformation. Communications is the cornerstone of a successful business transformation management plan, and a Communication Planning Tool allows greater degrees of awareness, planning and thought into this critical area.

Question 3 Do you have a process to manage shortfalls, issues, and escalations?

Condition: Absolutely Somewhat Not Yet Not Sure Not Required

Observation: Caution. Your feedback suggests that you do not have adequate processes in place to manage shortfalls, issues and escalations. This could be an area of exposure. It is important to recognize that these are key indicators of concern, which must be addressed. Without the processes in place to manage shortfalls, issues and escalations, your project has a very large exposure because you won't be able to close these issues consistently or track them to capture trends which must be addressed.

> "A culture of discipline is not just about action. It is about getting disciplined people who engage in disciplined thought and who then take disciplined action"
>
> – Jim Collins[5]

Managing shortfalls indicates that your project has the checks and balances in place to know when you are missing a deadline, a deliverable may not be as complete as required, or any thing else, which causes your project to fall short of plan. There are usually many causes, and your process must find the root cause for the shortfall, correct the cause, and put the controls in place to ensure it doesn't happen again. Managing issues indicates that you have a process to acknowledge an issue, track the issue, and develop and implement a solution to the issue. Managing escalations means that, as these are received, you have a process to acknowledge receipt, track the escalation, direct it to the owner, implement the corrective action, notify the initiator, and close the escalation. By tracking issues and escalations, you will be able to recognize any trends that may be developing that require a more in-depth solution.

It is extremely important that you have a management process to resolve shortfalls, issues and escalations. You must manage all of these items to ensure a successful project plan and adherence to time lines.

Recommendation: Your follow-up should stress building and maintaining credibility that processes are in place to track and manage shortfalls, issues and escalations; that is:

- Ensure that you establish documented processes to manage shortfalls, issues and escalations. Key components of these processes include the following:
  - Documenting

Figure 9-3 Question 3 Action plan

| Develop processes to manage shortfalls, issues and escalations | → | Develop reporting that includes trending and management reports | → | Meet face to face quarterly with Key Stakeholders to review trending and ongoing performance |

[5] _Good to Great – Why Some Companies Make the Leap and Others Don't_ (Copyright 2001 by Jim Collins, Published by HarperCollins Publishers Inc., New York).

    - Acknowledging
    - Root Cause Corrective Action
    - Initiator Sign off (if necessary)
    - Tracking
    - Trending
    - Reporting
    - Management Review

- Ensure that the resolution signoff process is closely adhered to
- Ensure that all shortfalls, issues, and escalations are captured and resolved
- Ensure Project Plan captures these new milestones and adjusts time lines as necessary

Actions: An iterative approach, as shown below in flow-charted form, will allow you to define and implement processes to track, manage and report shortfalls, issues, and escalations within your project team and with key stakeholders.

Support Tools: The implementation of issues and escalation processes are critical enablers to any project management effort. Any large, complex and time focused project will find itself challenged by things that do not go as planned; assumptions that are proven wrong; or conflicting priorities from other important initiatives. What separates a successful project from less successful ones is how those issues are found, communicated, managed, and eliminated or mitigated. Successful project management teams understand that issues will arise, and that they are a normal product of the change process. Note also, that in some organizations, the issue and escalation management processes are part of the input and status activity for their Quality Management reporting system.

Issue management and escalation processes should possess the following attributes:

- Clear ownership and accountability to manage the process.
- Widespread understanding of the process by the project team.
- Means to easily use, and receive statuses from, the process.
- Means to uniquely identify an issue including type, originator, date originated, current status, priority level, and notes.
- Means to assign items to appropriate personnel, and to track resolution and status.
- Means to provide feedback to originating person regarding status and then, if closed, the resulting root cause and solution implemented.

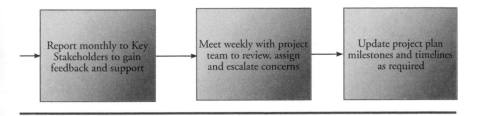

- Regular Executive Sponsorship review of all issues and escalations.
- Executive Sponsorship behavior that promotes, rather than discourages, use of the process; that is, "Better to know now rather than fail later!"
- Assignment of goals to appropriate personnel to manage, track and resolve issues and escalations in a timely manner.
- Development and communication of a policy designed to drive the appropriate behaviors and actions.

Tracking - Issue and escalation management tracking is critical to implementing a process that drives the desired results. Tracking methods should include the following:

- A system of record that manages all current and historical items.
- Clear definition of the originator including means to status them.
- Unique item identifier. An example is an identifier "040325_OM_001" where "040325" is YYMMDD; "OM" is the acronym for the given process where failure occurred; and, "001" is the issue or escalation item as assigned by the tracking system.
- An ability to assign a priority level to the issue or escalation
- An ability to assign ownership and track resolution activities.
- A reporting mechanism to assist Project and Executive Management with the ability to drive the desired behavior.
- A communication process to enable project members to focus regularly on solving issues.

Resolution - *Resolution management* is critical to implementing a process that drives the desired results. Management methods should include the following:

- A system of record that manages all current and historical items.
- Clear definition of the resolution owner including latest status, priority and planned resolution activities.
- Ability to reassign tasks or item in the event resolution is more appropriately handled by other skill set or resource.
- Ability to report time-based, threshold reporting either proactively or reactively; that is, the number of days past-due, or the number of days until target resolution.
- Reporting mechanism to assist Project and Executive Management with the ability to drive the desired behavior.
- Assignment of *goals* to appropriate personnel to drive resolution activity
- Reporting mechanism to assist Project and Executive Management with the ability to drive the desired behavior.
- Assignment of goals to appropriate personnel to drive resolution activity within the policy timeframes per the resolution type and priority.
  within the policy timeframes per the resolution type and priority.

Closed Loop - A *closed loop process* is critical to implementing a process that drives the desired results in the organization. This process allows the originator to see that their comments, actions and initiative matters. Closed loop processing should include the following:

- A system of record that allows for easy and complete initiation of issues and escalations.
- A system of record that records specific information about the originator so that status can be provided.
- A system of record that provides status to originators of issues and escalations.
- A process that recognizes the importance of issue and escalation

identification and submissions.

- Assignment of goals to appropriate personnel to drive closed loop processing of all activity within the policy timeframes per the resolution type and priority.

Question 4 Do you have the program management skills and resources to deliver this effort?

Condition: Absolutely   Somewhat   Not Yet | Not Sure | Not Required

Observations:

Caution. Your feedback suggests that you may not have the program management skills or resources available to support your change program. It is important to understand the importance of these skills and resources to your project.

The program management skills that are required to manage a change project are very complex and mature. They require handling of multiple milestones being supported by internal and external resources. Constant communication, milestone checks and statuses must be coordinated and evaluated. Informing the key stakeholders on a regular basis is extremely important. Managing the cost envelope and tracking the Return On Investment (ROI) are also important.

Program management resources typically fall into two categories, personnel and tools. It is important that the program management personnel have the correct skills and experience to support your change project. It is also important that the right program management tools are available and utilized. There are many tools in this area that will work sufficiently. The best tools are the ones that can be accessed by multiple resources so that updates are made on a timely basis.

If the program management skills and resources are not available, it will be extremely difficult to execute and implement a successful project plan.

Recommendation: With these observations in mind, taking the following steps to define and obtain commitments for your program management requirements are critical:

- Understand the program management skills and resources that are required to manage your change project.
- Determine where there are gaps and take action to fill those gaps.
- Continuously update and engage your resources in every aspect of the project.
- Have a well thought out documented process plan for all processes including each phase of the project, sign off authority, escalation path, and project plan with time lines and milestones.
- Have a clear and concise method of communication to and from your resources.
- Provide regular and timely updates to all Stakeholders.

Actions: An approach, as shown below in flow-charted form, will allow you to map out, align and communicate your program management skill and resource requirements with your key stakeholders, and provide an iterative process to address changes as you progress.

Figure 9-4 Question 4 Action plan

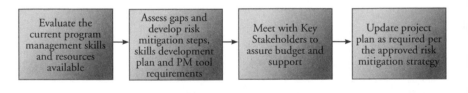

Support Tools: An *Action Plan* is a short-term plan, which highlights an area of concern, action items which will address the area of concern, time line, and resource requirements. This plan is presented to Management, and is then used to track the actions necessary to eliminate the area of concern to closure. These planned actions may also be called a Corrective Action Plan, which is generally used to define a process to eliminate the cause of a detected nonconformity and, in some instances, multiple non conformities.

Corrective action is taken to prevent recurrence. Correction relates to containment whereas corrective action relates to the root cause. A corrective action plan should include a short-term fix to ensure that the current process is prevented from further risk or exposure. Additionally, a long-term cost/risk weighted action, based upon an understanding of the product or process involved, should be taken to prevent the problem from reoccurring.

The corrective action plan can also address inadequate "conditions", which may produce a nonconformance. In this application, the corrective action plan should include root cause analysis and process change directions to correct the nonconformity, and possibly data indicating the current and future potential exposure to the nonconformity as well.

Question 5 Do you thoroughly understand the enabler processes required to obtain and utilize the project resources?

Condition: Absolutely   Somewhat   Not Yet   Not Sure   Not Required

Observations: Danger. Your feedback suggests that it is not necessary that you understand the enabling processes to obtain and utilize the resources needed for your change project. If you are in a small to mid-size business, and have an Executive Management mandate to move forward with your project, then you are likely okay to proceed. If this is not the case, then you must understand that each subcomponent of your project could require a different process to be completed.

Your project requires overall Executive Management and stakeholder approval. This would include a budget, which must be supported through the Finance team and planned into your company's Medium Range Plan (MRP). Capital equipment typically follows its own approval process that also involves Finance support and MRP inclusion. Internal Headcount resources will need to be allocated, which will require management approval, and may possibly include training to support the coverage model. External headcount resources require the support of Finance as well as a headcount requisition or consultant contract, which must be approved and budgeted. Information Technology will need to determine what additional resources they will need to support your project, and to maintain current development and support programs. Here again, this could require headcount resource additions, but in a different department.

In this scenario, you need to understand what processes must be completed to secure your projects resources. They must be accounted for in your project milestones and time line.

Recommendation: Review whether you have an Executive Management mandate or if you must go through the enabling processes to secure your projects resources.

If *you do* have a mandate, then you must:

Figure 9-5 Question 5 Action plan

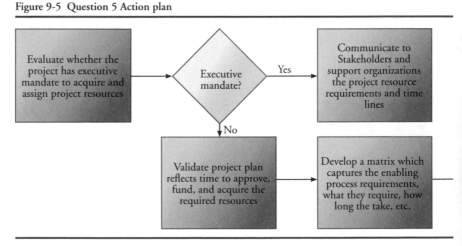

- Ensure all stakeholders are informed of the project resource requirements.
- Ensure all support functions are informed of the project resource requirements.
- Ensure Finance obtains budget allocation.

If you *do not* have a mandate, then you must:

- Ensure you account for the request, approval, budgeting and allocation time lines for each of the resources that are required for your team.
- Gather the written processes at your disposal in order to follow them correctly to minimize delays to all approval, budgeting and allocation requests.
- Ensure your project milestones and time lines correctly reflect the approval cycles and time requirements.
- Meet regularly with your project team, executive sponsors and stakeholders, to review the project plan and address any issues.

Actions: An iterative approach, as shown below in flow-charted form, will allow you to not only determine whether you have a *mandate* or not, but also allow you to define, communicate and obtain project resources if you do not.

Support Tools: A *Communication Planning Tool* is designed to assist management with a structured means to organize essential communications tasks in support of broad scale change in the business environment. The tool allows the user to identify various types of communications; the audience of those communications; who owns developing and delivering the communications; the appropriate method of delivery; and, the frequency of delivery. This tool also captures the expected outcome and due dates for the messaging.

A *Communication Planning Tool* also enables a methodical approach to communications such that the author can plan, and deliver, the communications with an increased probability of a successful outcome. An established approach enables confidence in communications, which will improve the likelihood that the targeted audiences will receive the required information in the intended timeframes to improve understanding, alignment, and adoption of the

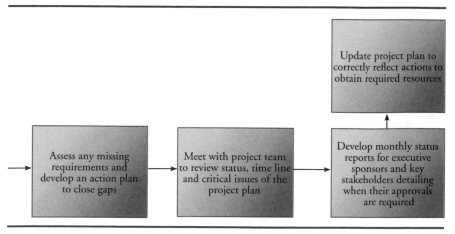

planned transformation. Communications is the cornerstone of a successful business transformation management plan, and a Communication Planning Tool allows greater degrees of awareness, planning and thought into this critical area.

ASSESSMENT IMPACT AND CHANGE IMPLEMENTATION

Depending up the project you are leading, there may be other outcomes in the area of action that must be assessed. The opportunity to add additional questions, which provide more insight and involve more preparation, is always an available option. Unique projects may require focused attention in the area of government approval or support, corporate policy changes, legal ramifications, or financial considerations to name a few. Areas like these may require their own questions that, in turn, must be assessed to ensure a successful change effort.

Once you've completed your assessment in the **Driving Complex Change®** element of action, you will understand your strengths as well as those areas that need an increased focus in order to successfully effect change. Expected outcomes include:

- Understanding if your project is approved, funded and resourced
- Understanding if a communication plan is in place
- Understanding if an escalation process is in place
- Identifying the Program Management skills available to your project
- Understanding the enabler processes required to support your project

By ensuring that key aspects of action are in place, you have enabled a key element which supports successful implementation of complex change within your organization or company.

PART III

Driving Complex Change® Application

In this part....

- Achieving Change Management Mastery
- Driving Complex Change® Integrated Applications
- Driving Complex Change® Business Impact

In Chapters 10 and 11, we will further review and tie the **Driving Complex Change®** methodology and underlying elements and tools together to not only show how they will predictably and reliably impact change management; but also, how applying this methodology as part of your overall business systems provides you with a robust and integrated approach to building the skills and capabilities you need to be successful over time.

> "An open organization is one that is designed to have constant, intense interactions with its external environments and to respond quickly and flexibly to new information. In an open organization, people share a set of norms, values, and priorities that contribute to learning-alertness to change, a search for new challenges and options, and respect for innovation and risk taking. An open organization is also future-oriented, in the sense that much of its behavior is governed by anticipation of future threats and opportunities and a concern for the future consequences of current strategies."
>
> – Warren Bennis and Burt Nanus[1]

---

[1] Leaders: The Strategies for Taking Charge (Harper and Row, 1985).

Becoming Masters of Change

Key topics covered in this chapter ....

- Achieving Change Mastery
- Review of Methodology and Underlying Concepts
- Application of the Methodology
    - ■ Assessment and Information - Current State
    - ■ Proposed Mitigation Action - Future State
    - ■ Planning Direction and Dimensions - Future State
    - ■ Tools that Facilitate - Future State
    - ■ Change Implementation Capability and Readiness

"Coming together is a beginning; keeping together is progress; working together is success."

- Henry Ford

INTRODUCTION

In the preceding chapters we explored the many facets of change, the constancy of change, and the practicality of the **Driving Complex Change®** methodology.

Thus far you should have a sense of the following:

- A detailed explanation of the six **Driving Complex Change®** elements.
- The value proposition available from focusing on each element for a given change initiative within your business.
- How you can derive practical value from assessing your change initiative from a specific set of considerations.
- The interrelationship between the element assessment activity and the underlying framework of Observations, Recommendations and Actions (ORA).
- How applying the specific recommendations and actions, and using the supporting tools can promote the efficient and effective impact you desire for your initiative.

In this chapter, we will tie the **Driving Complex Change®** methodology together and recap how each element fits together, like the cylinders of an engine, accelerating you effectively and efficiently towards your change goals. We will further explore how the many underlying tools can be utilized to help steer your team and remove the many bumps that are a normal part of any road to success.

We will further explain the business landscape and where applying the **Driving Complex Change®** methodology can assist a business in assessing the distance a project has traveled, and whether the path chosen is having the desired effect on business performance.

Finally, we will tie these elements and underlying tools together to show how applying the **Driving Complex Change®** methodology is essential to predictably and reliably improving the change effectiveness factors expressed in the $Q \times A = E$ relationship, and, that by doing so, a business can effect change quickly and efficiently to enable a competitive advantage.

ACHIEVING CHANGE MASTERY

Let's take a moment to refresh ourselves with an overview of the **Driving Complex Change®** methodology. We have explained that the **Driving Complex Change®** methodology is a set of interrelated and mutually dependent elements, illustrated in Figure 10.1, for managing successful change. We then declared that, by understanding and using this methodology to focus on the six key areas of a project, program, product or other change initiative, you will note a profound impact on the ability of your organization to affect change and, subsequently, business success. Furthermore, by applying the underlying concepts involved, we said that you will notice remarkable improvements in the areas of quality, the ability to adopt and implement new practices, and in overall time to implement. The results will be realized with increased Customer Satisfaction and improved Shareholder Maximization.

Figure 10.1   Benefits of Driving Complex Change®

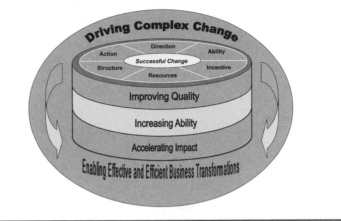

REVIEW OF METHODOLOGY AND UNDERLYING CONCEPTS

Using the analogy of an engine, let's consider each of the six elements of the Driving Complex Change® methodology as cylinders within that engine. For an engine to perform efficiently, each cylinder must be clean and free of any deficiencies to efficiently and effectively convert the energy contained in the fuel into a locomotive force that moves the automobile forward. Understanding how each cylinder is constructed, and how cleaning that cylinder of any deposits makes a difference in how the engine performs, and enables you the driver, to get to your intended destination more effectively and efficiently.

Applying this analogy to the direction element, as a cylinder in a business change initiative, we can see how the areas of observations, recommendations and actions (ORA) complete the construction of this essential element. Each collection of observations, recommendations and actions are created specifically for the scope of that element. The following graphic (Figure 10.2) is for the direction element, but it should be understood that each Driving Complex Change® element has a similar construction.

Figure 10.2   Cross Sectional view: Driving Complex Change® and ORA Structure

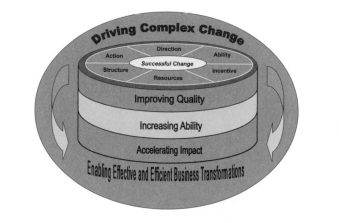

Once the change initiative is assessed and a completeness rating determined and recorded, we then develop performance ratings, which are the result of the variance between the actual performance level and the predetermined set of requirements and standards for that given change area.

Based upon the level of deviation of the observed value from the predetermined standard or norm, the **Driving Complex Change®** methodology proposes a set of recommendations and actions. A program or project team will then take those recommendations and schedule the completion of the proposed actions to mitigate any concerns or risks that might be apparent in that specific area or element.

Each element and corresponding set of observations, recommendations and "proposed" actions have a specific focus and scope. Together these provide the change initiative owner with a set of recommendations and actions to address any perceived gaps that may be observed.

This process repeats itself for each of the other five elements so that the ability of the program or project team to deliver a quality change initiative is improved as well as a higher probability of an effective or efficient outcome from the change initiative.

Let's review the scope and focus of each **Driving Complex Change®** element and regain a sense of what has been covered in the preceding chapters.

Direction as discussed in Chapter 4:

- Understanding the business value
- Executive Stakeholders alignment
- Team makeup identified
- Business advantages captured
- Shareholder Value defined

Ability as discussed in Chapter 5:

- Understanding your core competencies

- Identification of non core competency areas
- Understanding if core competencies support your Customer Value Proposition
- Understanding if core competencies tie to your capital investment strategies
- Assessing if an outsourcing plan exists and is valid

Incentive as discussed in Chapter 6:

- Understanding if defined goals and objectives are in place
- Understanding if goals and objectives are measurable and achievable (SMART)
- Identifying if an internal rewards system is in place and/or required
- Understanding the capabilities of the current measurement and reporting process
- Identifying if an external rewards system is in place and/or required

Resources as discussed in Chapter 7:

- Identifying your resource requirements
- Understanding if a resource plan is in place, approved and budgeted
- Understanding if you have the tools and skills to manage the required resources
- Identifying your communication methodology and plan
- Understanding if the required resources are available when you need them

Structure as discussed in Chapter 8:

- Understanding if a Quality Management System is in place
- Identifying existing internal Service Level Agreements
- Identifying the processes being considered for change
- Understanding if these processes are measured, goaled and rewarded on performance
- Understanding if a Systems Map is in place

Action as discussed in Chapter 9:

- Understanding if your project is approved, funded and resourced
- Understanding if a communication plan is in place
- Understanding if an escalation process is in place
- Identifying the Program Management skills available to your project
- Understanding the enabler processes required to support your project

APPLICATION OF THE METHODOLOGY

You may recall that we used the following scenario as a backdrop, in chapters 4 through 9, to show how applying the **Driving Complex Change®** methodology would create powerful information for managing a successful change initiative.

Scenario Example

"You have been designated as the Program Manger of a major restructuring effort within your company (ABC). In addition, ABC has just competed the acquisition of another company (XYZ). This effort will require integration of the newly acquired company into the current organizational structure. There are many stakeholders involved, some of whom are not in synch with the changes involved.

Product alignments, central to this acquisition, are solid, but there are clear cultural and operating style differences between the two organizations. Communications about this restructuring effort have been spotty and, as may be expected, many rumors have been circulating about job cuts and big changes. All this had led to levels of fear and uncertainty as to how individuals and functions will be impacted.

This project will include outsourcing specific functions that are not considered core competencies within the restructured company. Competencies to be retained or strengthened will need to be agreed upon and, in non-core areas, plans for divestment need to be developed.

You are currently on a small team that has HR and Finance members. Functions within ABC are unsure of what is required of them and whether they have the resources to address the rumored time lines.

Existing business practices have been partially documented and distributed, however, some undocumented practices do exist. There are also questions about the overall readiness of these practices to be moved to an outside provider. The processes involved will need to be institutionalized and measured to determine if the restructuring objectives and goals are being achieved.

Executive Management is expecting a game plan to ensure that a smooth, timely and successful organizational integration and related outsourcing effort will occur. A variety of e-mails have been exchanged between the management teams of both companies and expectations are currently unbounded. This lack of aligned focus within the teams makes building a restructuring plan for management approval and funding difficult."

The restructuring effort was evaluated using the **Driving Complex Change®** assessment methodology and the ORA based requirements and standards.

ASSESSMENT AND INFORMATION – CURRENT STATE

The following is a summary of the scope of observation information that was asked for during the **Driving Complex Change®** assessment process. With this information, expressed in terms of element-specific questions and categorized responses, you can gain an overall sense of where the project is and what gaps exist in its ability to successfully navigate the change.

Figure 10.3   Driving Complex Change® Assessment Example

Direction	1	Do you have Executive Stakeholder alignment and support?	Not Yet
	2	Do you have a cross-functional team to lead this effort?	Not Yet
	3	Will this decision increase shareholder value?	Not Yet
	4	Do you have an agreed upon vision and strategies defined to support change?	Not Sure
	5	Do your strategies map to your Customer Value Proposition?	Not Required
Ability	1	Do you have a process to understand and identify your core competencies?	Absolutely
	2	Do your core competencies support your Customer Value Proposition?	Somewhat
	3	Are your non-core competent areas well defined and measured for results?	Not Yet
	4	Do your core competencies tie to your capital investment strategies?	Not Sure
	5	Do you have an outsourcing plan for your non-core competent areas?	Not Required
Incentive	1	Have you defined the goals and objectives for this effort?	Absolutely
	2	Are these goals and objectives measurable and achievable?	Somewhat
	3	Do you have an internal reward system in place to support desired outcomes?	Not Yet
	4	Do you have a predictable and sustainable measurement and reporting process?	Not Sure
	5	Do you have an external reward system in place to support desired outcomes?	Not Required
Resources	1	Have you established a plan detailing all required resources (Head count, Capital, etc..)?	Absolutely
	2	Has your resource plan been approved by the Executive Stakeholders and is it being funded in the current budget?	Somewhat
	3	Do you have the tools and skills to manage the resources for this effort?	Not Yet
	4	Do you have a mechanism in place for communication and status reporting activities?	Not Sure
	5	Are the resources available for the timeframe that you require?	Not Required
Structure	1	Do you have a documented Quality Management System in place for all key processes and procedures?	Absolutely
	2	Do you have a Service Level Agreement with your internal providers?	Somewhat
	3	Do you have a thorough understanding of the processes that you are considering for change?	Not Yet
	4	Is today's process measured, goaled, and rewarded based upon performance?	Not Sure
	5	Do you have a documented information flow for systems capture?	Not Required
Action	1	Is your project approved, funded and resourced?	Absolutely
	2	Do you have a communication strategy to manage stakeholder's expectations?	Somewhat
	3	Do you have a process to manage shortfalls, issues and expectations?	Not Yet
	4	Do you have the program management skills and resources to deliver this effort?	Not Sure
	5	Do you thoroughly understand the enabler processes required to obtain and utilize the project resources (Capital Equipment, Head count, IT Development, Funding)?	Not Required

Using this approach, you will see how the current state of the change initiative can be diagnosed and given the required level of focus to close the gaps. Let's look at what information was actually generated as a result of the observation assessment, and what next steps we might consider in moving the change project forward.

The specific areas that have been observed as "Absolutely" are as follows:

- Process is in place to understand and identify your core competencies.
- Goals and objectives are defined.
- Resource plan is in place detailing head count, capital and other requirements.
- Quality Management system is in place for all key processes and procedures.
- Project is approved, funded and resourced.

Implication: The fact that the above has been observed as being in place is supportive in enabling the successful outcome of the change initiative.

The specific areas that have been observed as "Somewhat" are as follows:

- Core competencies support your Customer Value Proposition.
- Goals and objectives are measurable and achievable.
- Resource plan is approved and funded by the Executive Stakeholders.
- Service Level Agreements (SLA) is in place for your internal service providers.
- Communication strategy is in place to manage stakeholder's expectations.

Implication: The fact that the above has been observed as "Somewhat" in place supports and enables the successful outcome of the change initiative. However the ABC Program Manager for this change initiative should invest further time and effort in developing the end state of these attributes to a level where they are fully in place. Each area is a critical factor in the success of the change initiative.

The specific areas that have been observed as "Not Yet" are as follows:

- Executive Stakeholders are aligned and support the initiative.
- Cross-functional team is in place to lead this effort.
- Knowledge that the change initiative will increase shareholder value.
- Non-core competency areas are well defined and measured for results.
- Internal rewards system is in place to support desired results and behaviors.
- Tools and skills are available to manage the resources for this effort.
- A thorough understanding of the processes that you are considering for change.
- The existence of a process to manage shortfalls, issues and escalations.

Implication: While it is good that the state of these attributes is known and that you plan to get them in line, the fact is that they are not in place today and this is a concern for the change initiative. Efforts to address these concerns should be established immediately.

The specific areas that have been observed as "Not Sure" are as follows:

- Agreed upon vision and strategies for your change initiative.
- Core competencies tie to your capital investment strategies.   .
- Predictable and sustainable measurement and reporting process in place.
- Communication and status reporting mechanism in place.
- Today's process is measured, goaled and rewarded based upon performance.
- Program management skills and resources available to deliver this effort.

Implication: The inability to confirm the existence of these attributes within the change initiative is of an elevated concern for the project. It is best to invest more time to evaluate these areas and develop appropriate risk mitigations before proceeding.

The specific areas that have been observed as "Not Required" are as follows::

- Strategies map to your Customer Value Proposition.
- Existence of an Outsourcing Plan for you non core-competent areas.
- External rewards system in place to support desired outcomes.

- Resources available for the timeframe you require.
- Existence of a documented information flow for systems capture.
- Thorough understanding of the enabler processes required to obtain and utilize the project resources.

Implication: The evaluation of these attributes as "Not Required" is of significant concern for the ongoing success of the project. It is best to immediately invest time and effort to either complete these activities or gain Executive Stakeholder support for continuing the project without these attributes in place.

PLANNING DIRECTION AND DIMENSIONS – FUTURE STATE

The point of assessing change initiatives from the viewpoint of the **Driving Complex Change®** methodology is simply to utilize a set of industry best practices and company specific standards to drive programs to desired level of performance. With these practices and standards in hand, the ABC Program Manager will have the knowledge and insights necessary to understand what planning, communication and action areas must be in place, and when and at what level they must be in place to ensure program viability and success.

With the use of the **Driving Complex Change®** methodology, the ABC Program Manager increases their knowledge of the program by applying the diagnostic nature of the methodology to uncover gaps in the restructuring plans; that is, what is unavailable or not conforming to the level expected for this effort.

By using the **Driving Complex Change®** methodology, the ABC Program Manager now has information about the restructuring program that can be utilized to develop and implement risk mitigation plans. Using the automobile engine cylinder analogy again, the Program Manager now understands what is preventing or might prevent, the cylinders from effortlessly performing their duties.

PROPOSED MITIGATION ACTION – FUTURE STATE

We now can begin to see how using the observations, recommendations and actions (ORA) in the **Driving Complex Change®** methodology would further enhance the ABC Program Manager's ability to develop action plans that could proactively close the gaps present within a project.

The following diagrams show examples of the proposed mitigation actions that would be recommended to the Program Manager for those situations where the responses to the assessment questions were "Not Yet", "Not Sure" or "Not Required". Using these proposed actions, the Program Manager can then assess the appropriate next steps from which to close these gaps in observed performance.

The following are examples of the actions proposed for items where the assessment indicated a performance level of "Not Yet" are shown in graphic form:

Figure 10.4 Examples of Proposed Actions for Response on Not Yet

Direction	Will the decisions increase shareholder value? • Establish reviews to understand the complete expected impact on the stakeholder. • If impact is minimal and not clear why you would want to proceed, reprioritize effort as "nice to do". • If there is a time delay, ensure that you document the expected timeline to achieve shareholder value. Monitor progress and reassess as necessary.	Resources	Do you have the tools and skills to manage the resources for this effort? • Define the resources to achieve success. • Determine where the gaps exist in either the skills or tools to manage the resources. • Determine the best action to take in order to acquire the skills and tools to manage the project resources.
Ability	Are you non-core competent areas well defined and measured for results? • Identify your company's non-core competent areas. • Use this information to compare your non-core competent function to the industry experts of those functions to support your outsourcing decision making. • Establish well defined measure for your non-core competent areas.	Structure	Do you have a thorough understanding of the processes that you are considering for change? • Determine whether a Provider is going to use any of the existing processes. • If yes, all processes being utilized must be understood, documented and standardized. • If no, determine if a baseline must be established before moving forward and take appropriate action.

Incentive	Do you have an internal reward system in place to support desired outcomes?
	
	• Meet with key stakeholders and Finance to ensure that funding and approvals are in place for internal rewards system.
	• Ensure that the reward system in place is consistent and objective.
	• Ensure that the internal reward system is aligned with your desired outcome.
		Actions	Do you have a process to manage shortfalls, issues and escalations?
			
			• Ensure that you establish documented processes to manage shortfalls, issues and escalations. Key components of these processes include:
			   - Documenting
			   - Acknowledging
			   - Root Cause Corrective Action
			   - Initiator Sign Off
			   - Tracking

The following are examples of the actions proposed for items where the assessment indicated a performance level of "Not Sure" in graphic form:

Figure 10.5 Examples of Proposed Actions for Response on Not Sure

Direction	Do you have agreed upon vision and strategies defined to support change?
	
	 • Meet with Executive Stakeholders to confirm or establish the vision and strategies for the change effort and, upon agreement, assess the current situation and determine where gaps exist.
	  Resolve gaps and drive for resolution with Executive Stakeholders and upon final agreement continue to update over time.
		Resources	Do you have a mechanism in place for communication and status reporting activities?
			
			 • Review whether you have an effective communication mechanism in place.
			  If yes:
			  - Ensure that you have an effective communication plan in place.
			  - Ensure that key stakeholders, team members and cross-functional members are included

Ability	Do your core competencies tie to your capital investment strategies? • Ensure that your core competency areas are mapped and are part of the capital investment strategies (which leads to budget allocation process) to ensure continued investment. Address gaps that are found.	**Structure**	Is today's process measured, goaled and rewarded based upon performance? • Understand how the process is measured, goaled and if performance is rewarded. • If the process is measured, be sure to add those measures to the contract. If the process is not measured then develop measures, goals and performance rewards.
Incentive	Do you have a predictable and sustainable measurement and reporting process? • Determine what measurements and reporting processes must be put in place today that measures the process/function being targeted for change. • Ensure that your measurement and reporting processes maintain KPIs predictability and sustainability.	**Actions**	Do you have the program management skills and resources to deliver this effort? • Understand the Program Management skills and resources that are required to manage your change project. • Determine where there are gaps and take action to fill those gaps.

The following are examples of the actions proposed for items where the assessment indicated a performance level of "Not Required " in graphic form:

Figure 10.6 Examples of Proposed Actions for Response on Not Required

Direction	Do your strategies map to your Customer Value Proposition?	Resources	Are the resources available for the timeframe that you require?
	• Ensure that you meet with executive stakeholders to map your current strategies to your CVP. • Determine gaps and revise the strategies with the executive stakeholders. • Ensure that the revised strategies are communicated to stakeholders, project team members and support organizations.		• Review your resource plan. Understand whether there are any requirements for internal support of these resources. If so, determine if there are gaps and non-commitments which could derail your change project. • Develop an action plan to address any gaps. This could include securing internal and external resources.
Ability	Do you have an outsourcing plan for your non core competent areas?	Structure	Do you have a documented information flow for systems capture?
	• Assess if your company needs to develop an outsourcing plan for non core-competency areas. • If no, ensure that executive management understands the possible opportunities that exist in order to revisit this decision in the future.		• Ensure the scoring for the new support structure's systems and software capabilities is weighted correctly given the exposure this area represents to the change project. • Ensure that several super users evaluate the new support structure's capabilities in this area.
Incentive	Do you have an external reward system in place to support desired outcomes?	Actions	Do you thoroughly understand the enabler's process?
	• Research whether an external reward system is funded, and approved by your key stakeholders and Finance. • Evaluate the consistency and objectivity of external reward system in place. • Determine whether the external reward system is based on the desired outcomes with SMART goals and objectives.		• Review whether you have an Executive Management mandate or if you must go through the enabling processes to secure your project resources. • Ensure that all stakeholders are informed on the project resource requirements.

It should be noted that for purposes of brevity the above actions are only a subset of all the actions typically created and posted using the **Driving Complex Change®** assessment process.

Let's bring all this back into context. The ABC Program Manager was equipped with specific areas to assess for the restructuring-acquisition integration program. The project team then assessed the overall program using a predetermined set of questions focused on the availability of specific processes, practices and actions expected to be in place. Then the **Driving Complex Change®** methodology provided a set of observations, recommendations and actions based upon the project teams assessment.

Tools that Facilitate the Future State

The ABC Program Manager is now armed with the information of what and where the gaps are and what potential mitigation actions are available to proceed with a successful restructuring outcome. Some of these actions may be straightforward while others may be something the Program Manager has never experienced before. For the areas where there is no previous experience, how might the project team enable the actions and information necessary to fill the observed gaps? The answer is to utilize a set of tools specifically designed to address those areas.

Some examples of these tools include the following:

* SWOT tool: Provides a structured and methodical means to ascertain whether conditions within a given area of the business environment are a strength, weakness, opportunity or threat. With this viewpoint, management is equipped to develop appropriate strategies and goals to mitigate or capitalize on each area.

> "In many organizations there is more than a dim awareness that the performance audit [SWOT analysis] will turn over too many rocks, expose too many foibles, and raise issues about too many sacred cows to be comfortable or easy. Yet what is absolutely necessary in the performance audit is honesty and integrity. If defining one's future is one critical element of planning, another is knowing where one is starting from. "
>
> ~ Leonard Goodstein, Timothy Nolan and J. William Pfeiffer[1]

* Envision the Future tool: Captures the Vision, Mission, Strategies, Goals and Key Performance Indicators (KPIs) that are necessary to understand the value of the change initiative and it's alignment to the overall Customer Value Proposition.

> "Envisioning assumes that the organization has or is experiencing a need for transformation; that is, the organization now understands-at least on some level-that its future must be discontinuous from its past and present."
>
> ~ Leonard Goodstein, Timothy Nolan and J. William Pfeiffer[1]

* Core Competency tool: Focuses on understanding and assessing the business function's specific value proposition, and on assessing and implementing recommended actions to either invest or divest in that function's mid-to-long term viability within the business environment.

> "An effective mission statement will prevent people in the organization from developing and proposing many plans and projects that will not be accepted by top management, because they will be able to see that such plans or projects are not within the scope of the mission statement."
>
> ~ Leonard Goodstein, Timothy Nolan and J. William Pfeiffer[1]

* Stakeholder Assessment tool: Develops a viewpoint on the various groups that are required to support and/or will be impacted by the change initiative. The tool allows the user to assess the current state of support, determine the desired level of support, and then develop and assign actions to manage any gaps found.

---

[1] Applied Strategic Planning - How to Develop a Plan That Really Works (McGraw-Hill Publishers, 1993).

> "A vision cannot be established in an organization by edict, or by the exercise of power or coercion... But if the organization is to be successful, the image must grow out of the needs of the entire organization and must be "claimed" or "owned" by all the important actors."
>
> – Warren Bennis and Bert Nnus[2]

- **Communications Planning tool:** Communication is the single most important aspect of any successful change initiative. With the Communications Planning tool, you are equipped with the ability to determine, plan and manage what and when communications are required to be implemented, how best they will be delivered, by whom, and so forth. With this tool you are equipped to provide those affected by the initiative with the information they need to understand their specific role in supporting your project.

> "Leaders understand that unless they communicate and share information with their constituents, few will take much interest in what is going on. Unless people see and experience the effects of what they do, they won't care. When leaders share information rather than guard it, people feel included and respected."
>
> – Jim Kouzes and Barry Posner[3]

- **Risk Assessment tool:** The key to successful change is to understand the impact of quality, time and risk aversion on an initiative. As an example, it should be fairly well understood that it takes more time to design a product to a 100% level of quality rather than a level below 80%. The time is takes to go from 60% to 80% is not linearly equal to the time it takes to go from 80% to 90%, or 90% to 100%. With the Risk Assessment tool, you have available the means to capture all the risks noted and to assess the impact of those risks on your change initiative. The tool can be utilized with other tools such as the Stakeholder Assessment tool or Core Competency tool so that any apparent risks from those actions are captured and addressed.

- **Project Management tool:** Any complex change initiative has many actions taking place simultaneously. With the Project Management tool, the change initiative owner can manage all the actions necessary to ensure the optimal level of success. What makes this tool useful is that it can be integrated with other tools such that any actions derived elsewhere are captured and managed in one area.

> "You can either take action, or you can hang back and hope for a miracle. Miracles are great, but they are so unpredictable."
>
> – Peter Drucker[4]

Each of these tools has a specific focus and scope. By applying these tools, the ABC Program Manager is able to methodically and purposefully assess and facilitate the changes desired in the program.

The result is a change initiative whereby the following areas are completely understood, managed and enabled by establishing:

- Linkage between the change initiative scope and the businesses vision, mission, strategies and goals.
- Expected level of completion and scope of all Program Management process requirements.
- Knowledge of the variances in actual versus expected level of completeness for all facets of the change initiative.

---

[2] Leaders: The strategies for taking charge (Harper and Row, 1985).

[3] Credibility: How Leaders Gain and Lost It, Why People Demand It (Jossey-Blass, Inc Publishers, 1993).

[4] In To Your Success compiled by Dan Zadra and designed by Kobi Yamada and Steve Potter (Copyright 1997 by Compendium, Inc., Published by Compendium, Inc. Publishing and Communications – Edmonds, WA).

- Industry proven mitigation strategies and practices to use in shoring up gaps in performance.
- An ongoing assessment vehicle to use during all key milestones of the program.

CHANGE IMPLEMENTATION CAPABILITY AND READINESS

With the power of the **Driving Complex Change**® standardized assessments, gap analysis, action planning, integrated and structured tools, and closed loop performance management, the ABC Program Manager is quickly able to see the following implementation opportunities in support of the organization restructuring-XYZ acquisition effort.

- Stratification and grouping of Stakeholders.
- Completion of a core competency analysis to understand how best to fund the functions being acquired and merged.
- Instituting a methodical and robust process for outsourcing non-core competency activities.
- Completing a Vision, Strategy and Values mapping process to align all new, and existing, members into the ongoing business culture.
- Instituting a complete communications plan that incorporates and considers what needs to be communicated, to whom, when, how, and why.
- Business Process documentation assessment and Quality Management System planning.
- Development of a cross functional team that includes the appropriate mix of functional constituents to develop the participation, support and "buy-in" for the change initiative.
- Development of a complete integration plan, which is bounded and phased to deliver the required results over time.
- Development and management of an implementation plan that includes a close loop corrective action plan for ongoing mitigation of risks, concerns and issues that may arise.

By utilizing the **Driving Complex Change**® methodology, the project team is armed for success. They can now step into the unknown of the restructuring effort confident of success knowing that they are equipped with industry best practices, time proven actions, supporting tools and the power of information.

Epilogue

Key topics covered in this chapter ....

- Driving Complex Change® Overview
- The Path of Business Change
- Applying the Driving Complex Change® Methodology
- Why Businesses Must Master Change

"Though no one can go back and make a brand new start, anyone can start from now and make a brand new ending."

- Carl Bard

DRIVING COMPLEX CHANGE® OVERVIEW

Employing the **Driving Complex Change®** methodology improves the capacity to manage the multitude of complex interactions within the detailed areas of any change initiative.

Recapping how the elements of direction, ability, incentive, resources, structure, and action interact with the observations, recommendations and actions (ORA), we now see how focusing on the specific elements and assessing the completeness of specific areas within those elements, and applying the ORA technology can improve the change initiatives capability of success.

Figure 11-1   Driving Complex Change® Methodology Overview

Elements	Questions	Conditions	ORA
Direction	Question 1	Absolutely	Observation
	Question 2	Somewhat	
Ability	Question 3	Not Yet	Recommendation
	Question 4	Not Sure	
Incentive	Question 5	Not Required	Actions
Resources			
Structure			
Action			

With the **Driving Complex Change®** methodology and supporting tools, the project team is able to clearly view all the critical areas with a level of specificity that improves the probability of success. This new view becomes very broad and very deep across the change initiative. Some of the areas that would be observed and that recommendations and actions developed for, include the following:

- Understanding the business value
- Impact to Shareholders
- Executive Stakeholders alignment
- Program/Project Team construction and functional participation
- Core competency assessments
- Core competencies alignment to Customer Value Proposition
- Core competencies alignment to capital investment strategies
- Outsourcing plan capabilities assessment
- Defined goals and objectives in place
- Goals and objectives are measurable and achievable
- Internal Rewards System capability and impact
- Capability assessment of current measurement and reporting process
- Value of an External Rewards System
- Identification of Resource Requirements
- Resource Plan completeness and support
- Tools and skills capability assessment
- Communication plan completeness
- Project Plan completeness
- Funding and support of Resource and Project Plans
- Quality Management System capability
- Internal Service Level Agreements (SLAs) capability
- Technology and Business System assessment

- Availability of critical capability such as communication plans, escalation plans, project support and approvals, Program or Project Management effectiveness

The results will be a more deliberate focus yielding more teamwork, reduced waste, higher productivity, and a clearer view of what needs to be accomplished, which reduces time and provides fewer false starts and lower cost.

By assessing a program or project from these viewpoints, we trust that you can now see how managing from the capabilities contained within the **Driving Complex Change®** methodology would positively effect your ability to improve the impact of your project.

The result would be improvements in awareness and structure, the ability to complete the task at hand, a method to foster the behaviors required, less frustration and more excitement, an overall ease of moving ahead, and specific actions from which everyone can see the path to success.

The overall result would be a change initiative that is poised to obtain the full potential from the given change.

Tuning up your automobile (or business) with the **Driving Complex Change®** methodology enables you to drive quickly and uneventfully towards your change destination. With the **Driving Complex Change®** methodology in your "fuel tank" you can be rest assured that your project team's efforts can be trusted to develop the intended results, improve the quality of the initiative, and increase the ability or agility of the organization to adopt, accept or advance the initiative, thus achieving the resulting effect or impact of the change in terms of the productivity or customer value produced.

Figure 11.2   Misaligned Element Negative Impacts

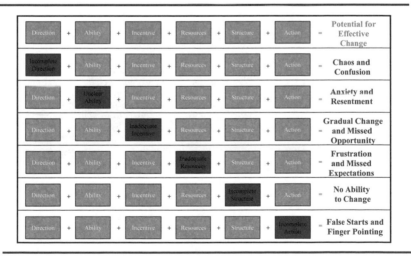

Going back to the automobile engine analogy used in Chapter 10, it is pretty common for businesses to have some of the cylinders working effectively and efficiently, however, the real opportunity is to have them all working together to derive the most impact. Applying the **Driving Complex Change®** methodology and resultant practices increases your capacity and capability to do just that and to impact each of the change effectiveness areas of the **Q x A = E** relationship.

With the **Driving Complex Change®** methodology not only do you get the ability to extend your knowledge of where and why to focus your efforts, but you also see how to focus for maximum efficiency and effectiveness.

THE PATH OF BUSINESS CHANGE

There are many specific and unique areas where you might apply the **Driving Complex Change®** methodology. These areas might range from designing and implementing a new product, a new process, or a new vision for your business, or, as in our scenario example, an organization restructuring-acquisition integration effort that the ABC business has undertaken.

In any situation, the overall plan for the change can be expressed using the following flow-charted example.

Figure 11.3   Plan for Change

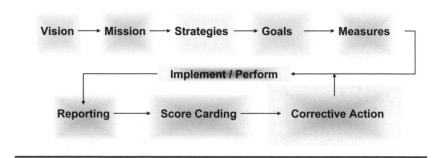

For any given change, there must be alignment between the initiative undertaken and the overall vision and mission of the business or organization. Once this is accomplished the development and implementation of specific strategies, goals and measures are essential to create a map of how the initiative will be accomplished. After the map is in place, there must then be a means to assess progress, understand deviations and then focus on overcoming any obstacles along the path to success. This is the underlying context and premise from which businesses apply the **Driving Complex Change®** methodology.

Applying the **Driving Complex Change®** methodology enables a business to address the following tasks:

- Define a set of required behaviors and standards that the project teams can then use proactively to enable successful change.
- Define a sound business plan describing the methods from which success is most probable.
- Define the strategies, which assert the best path to success.
- Define the goals by which the business will measure success over time.
- Assess current performance, against those standards, from the viewpoints of direction, ability, incentive, resources, structure and actions.
- Develop awareness and knowledge as to how best to allocate precious resources to address potential issues, gaps and deviations from expected performance levels.
- Increase predictability and reliability of managing change in all projects.
- Implement a structured and ongoing assessment and closed loop corrective action plan to continuously improve performance and results.

The robust nature of the **Driving Complex Change®** methodology creates a preventive maintenance plan for your business that can preempt and mitigate any conditions that might lead to initiative failure.

From this vantage point, a program or project manager can assess the gaps and develop a plan focused on what items or areas need to be addressed, in what priority, and how these gaps must be managed and closed.

This typically means bringing a collection of the following tools and processes to the project:
- Core Competency Analysis
- Vision and Strategy Development
- Goal and KPI development
- Risk Management
- Stakeholder Assessment
- Communications Planning
- Internal and External Score-carding
- Project and Program Management
- Closed Loop Corrective Action Management
- Budgeting and Resource Planning

While many change initiatives utilize some or all of these tools and processes, there is a unique opportunity to use the **Driving Complex Change®** methodology in an integrated manner with these tools and processes, which minimizes redundant management and processing of information.

In addition, with the **Driving Complex Change®** methodology, you can be assured that your efforts will target the critical areas of Quality (Q) and Acceptance (A), which positively impact the Effectiveness (E) of your project.

Not only will the efforts result in a higher quality product, program or project, but you will also impact your business's ability to deliver, accept, advance and adopt the change initiative which, taken together, will combine to improve the overall impact you desire.

APPLYING THE DRIVING COMPLEX CHANGE®
METHODOLOGY

There are many benefits of applying the **Driving Complex Change®** methodology in your business. With this methodology, your business gains a robust and integrated business practice that affords you the skills and capabilities needed to be successful.

The **Driving Complex Change®** methodology is also a very customizable and flexible framework that has many applications. Using this methodology as part of your business system, allows you to instill and institute standards in a variety of areas. Some examples of these areas include the following:

- *Business Performance Management* - The management and control of performance as it relates to specific business processes and functions.
- *Business Relationship Management* - The management of relationships between Providers-Company, Inter-Company and Company-Customer/Client engagements.
- *Business Transformation Management* - The management of change initiatives impacting the current and future state of business operations or practices.

CLOSING - WHY BUSINESSES MUST MASTER CHANGE

Change is all around us. Successful businesses must constantly change in order to meet customer requirements and maintain a competitive advantage.

> "It does not matter whether a change is originally seen as positive or negative; when people's expectations are significantly disrupted, the end result is resistance."
>
> - Daryl R. Conner[1]

The companies that master change management have a greater opportunity for success in the marketplace. The **Driving Complex Change®** methodology provides your company a cost effective and systemic path to mastering change.

---

[2] <u>Managing At The Speed Of Change - How Resilient Managers Succeed and Prosper Where Others Fail</u> (Villard Books Publishers, 1992).

Appendices

Driving Complex Change®

In this part....

- Company Profile
- Bibliography
- Glossary
- Index

COMPANY OVERVIEW

 ASIL, Inc.

Businesses today are expected to respond quickly to both external and internal changes while maintaining or increasing their level of performance. This typically requires the involvement of external forces to insure the adoption and successful implementation of the new processes or practices. The decision to implement structural change to an organization is executed with the greatest intent to achieve a desired end-result. Successful results will demand constant communication and monitoring to ensure that all parties are aligned and engaged, and that all issues are being resolved.

ASIL Inc. is a consulting company with solutions targeted at increasing business performance. We provide software and consulting solutions based upon industry leading best practices to enable companies to solve complex problems in areas like: change management, outsourcing, score carding and closed loop corrective action resolution. Each area is supported by a suite of integrated web based tools to achieve your business objectives, i.e., strategic clarity, increased productivity, cost reduction, SOX compliance, etc. . We provide economic and scalable solutions that have instant start-up capabilities and require no IT infrastructure.

Our approach at ASIL, Inc. is to enable and accelerate Business Performance within your company. We offer solutions in the following areas:

- **Business Transformation Management** - Provides a suite of Change Management tools to assist you in organizational changes and program management.

- **Business Relationship Management** – Facilitates process controls and sets stage for all of your outsourcing requirements so that you can electronically engage prospective partners on engagements.

- **Corporate Performance Management** – Delivers visibility and governance for all active processes and providers through score cards, dashboards, and a closed loop action/resolution process.

We have assembled an award winning team that delivers products and consulting services to increase your overall business performance and profitability. Experience the competitive advantage that MAX Partnering® will provide to your organization.

Contact sales@asil-inc.com or
ASIL, Inc. 2901 Tasman Drive, Suite 117, Santa Clara, CA 95054
(480) 980-9904 www.asil-inc.com

BIBLIOGRAPHY

FOREWORD

1 Ed Oakley and Doug Krug, <u>Enlightened Leadership - Getting to the Heart of Change</u> (Simon & Schuster, New York, 1st ed. 1993).

2 Leonard Goodstein, Timothy Nolan and J. William Pfeiffer, <u>Applied Strategic Planning - How to Develop a Plan That Really Works</u> (McGraw-Hill Publishers, 1993).

PART 1: CHANGE AND CHANGE MANAGEMENT

1 Peter Senge, Art Kleiner, Charlotte Roberts, Richard Ross, George Roth and Bryan Smith, <u>The Dance of Change - The Challenges to Sustaining Momentum in Learning Organizations</u> (Doubleday Publishers, 1999).

CHAPTER 1: CHANGE IN THE WORK PLACE

1 John P. Kotter and Dan S, Cohen, <u>The Heart of Change</u> (Copyright 2002, John P.Kotter and Deloitte Consulting LLC, Harvard Business School Publishing).

2 Ed Oakley and Doug Krug, <u>Enlightened Leadership - Getting to the Heart of Change</u> (Fireside Publishers, 1991).

3 Leonard Goodstein, Timothy Nolan and J. William Pfeiffer, <u>Applied Strategic Planning - How to Develop a Plan That Really Works</u> (McGraw-Hill Publishers, 1993).

4 Jim Kouzes and Barry Posner, <u>Credibility: How Leaders Gain and Lost It, Why People Demand It</u> (Jossey-Blass Inc. Publishers, 1993).

CHAPTER 2: CHANGE MANAGEMENT METHODOLOGY

1 John P. Kotter and Dan S, Cohen, <u>The Heart of Change</u> (Copyright 2002, John P.Kotter and Deloitte Consulting LLC, Harvard Business School Publishing, Boston, MA).

2 Ed Oakley and Doug Krug, <u>Enlightened Leadership - Getting to the Heart of Change</u> (Fireside Publishers, 1991).

CHAPTER 3: DRIVING COMPLEX CHANGE® - APPLICATION

No quotes listed.

PART 2: DRIVING COMPLEX CHANGE® CONCEPTS, METHODS, AND PRACTICES

1 Leonard Goodstein, Timothy Nolan, and J. William Pfeiffer, <u>Applied Strategic Planning - How to Develop a Plan That Really Works</u> (McGraw-Hill Publishers, 1993).

CHAPTER 4: DIRECTION ELEMENT – FOCUS AND ANALYSIS

1 Leonard Goodstein, Timothy Nolan, and J. William Pfeiffer, <u>Applied Strategic Planning - How to Develop a Plan That Really Works</u> (McGraw-Hill Publishers, 1993).

2 Daryl R. Conner, <u>Managing At The Speed Of Change - How Resilient Managers Succeed and Prosper Where Others Fail</u> (Villard Books Publishers 1992).

3 Daryl R. Conner, <u>Managing At The Speed Of Change - How Resilient Managers Succeed and</u>

Prosper Where Others Fail (Villard Books Publishers, 1992).

4 Katherine Catlin and Jana Mathews, Leading at the Speed of Growth (Copyright 2001, Kauffman Center for Entrepreneurial Leadership, Ewing Marion Kauffman Foundation, Published by Hungry Minds Inc., New York).

5 Ed Oakley and Doug Krug, Enlightened Leadership - Getting to the Heart of Change (Fireside Publishers, 1991}.

CHAPTER 5: ABILITY ELEMENT – FOCUS AND ANALYSIS

1 Katherine Catlin and Jana Matthews, Learning at the Speed of Growth (Hungry Minds, Inc. Publishers, 2001).

2 Leonard Goodstein, Timothy Nolan, and J. William Pfeiffer, Applied Strategic Planning - How to Develop a Plan That Really Works (McGraw-Hill Publishers, 1993).

3 Cathleen Benko and F. Warren McFarlan, Connecting the Dots - Aligning Projects with Objectives in Unpredictable Times (Harvard Business School Publishing, 2003).

4 Benjamin Gomes-Casseres, The Alliance Revolution - The New Shape of Business Rivalry (First Harvard University Press 1996).

CHAPTER 6: INCENTIVE ELEMENT – FOCUS AND ANALYSIS

1 Cathleen Benko and F. Warren McFarlan, Connecting the Dots - Aligning Projects with Objectives in Unpredictable Times (Harvard Business School Publishing, 2003).

CHAPTER 7: RESOURCES ELEMENT – FOCUS AND ANALYSIS

1 Cathleen Benko, and F. Warren McFarlan, Connecting the Dots - Aligning Projects with Objectives in Unpredictable Times (Harvard Business School Publishing, 2003).

CHAPTER 8: STRUCTURE ELEMENT – FOCUS AND ANALYSIS

1 Katherine Catlin and Jana Mathews, Leading at the Speed of Growth (Copyright 2001, Kauffman Center for Entrepreneurial Leadership, Ewing Marion Kauffman Foundation).

2 Katherine Catlin and Jana Matthews, Building the Awesome Organization – Six Essential Components that Drive Entrepreneurial Growth (Copyright 2002 Kauffman Center for Entrepreneurial Leadership, Ewing Marion Kauffman Foundation, Published by Hungry Minds Inc.)

3 Peter Senge, Art Kleiner, Charlotte Roberts, Richard Ross, George Roth and Bryan Smith, The Dance of Change - The Challenges to Sustaining Momentum in Learning Organizations (Doubleday Publishers, 1999}.

4 Peter M. Senge, The Fifth Discipline - The Art and Practice of The Learning Organization (Doubleday Publishers, 1990}.

CHAPTER 9: ACTION ELEMENT – FOCUS AND ANALYSIS

1 In To Your Success, compiled by Dan Zadra and designed by Kobi Yamada and StevePotter (Copyright 1997 by Compendium, Inc.,Published by Compendium, Inc. Publishing and Communications, Edmonds, WA).

2 In To Your Success, compiled by Dan Zadra and designed by Kobi Yamada and StevePotter

(Copyright 1997 by Compendium, Inc.,Published by Compendium, Inc. Publishing and Communications, Edmonds, WA).

3 John P. Kotter and Dan S, Cohen, <u>The Heart of Change</u> (Copyright 2002 John P.Kotter and Deloitte Consulting LLC, Harvard Business School Publishing).

4 <u>Good to Great – Why Some Companies Make the Leap and Others Don't</u>, Jim Collins (Copyright 2001 by Jim Collins, Published by HarperCollins Publishers Inc,, New York).

PART 3: DRIVING COMPLEX CHANGE® APPLICATION AND IMPACT

1 Warren Bennis and Burt Nanus, <u>Leaders: The Strategies for Taking Charge</u> (Harper and Row, 1985).

CHAPTER 10: BRINGING IT ALL TOGETHER

1 Leonard Goodstein, Timothy Nolan and J. William Pfeiffer, <u>Applied Strategic Planning - How to Develop a Plan That Really Works </u>(McGraw-Hill Publishers, 1993).

2 Warren Bennis and Bert Nnus, <u>Leaders: The Strategies For Taking Charge</u> (Harper and Row, 1985).

3 Jim Kouzes and Barry Posner, <u>Credibility: How Leaders Gain and Lost It, Why People Demand It</u> (Jossey-Blass, Inc Publishers, 1993).

4 <u>In To Your Success</u> compiled by Dan Zadra and designed by Kobi Yamada and Steve Potter (Copyright 1997 by Compendium, Inc., Published by Compendium, Inc. Publishing and Communications – Edmonds, WA).

CHAPTER 11: EPILOGUE

1 Daryl R. Conner, <u>Managing At The Speed Of Change - How Resilient Managers Succeed and Prosper Where Others Fail</u> (Villard Books Publishers, 1992).

GLOSSARY

Business Transformation Management (BTM)

Business Transformation Management (BTM) refers to a method of management focus, designed to enable Business's to implement effective and efficient change programs, that benefit all stakeholders involved (client, employee, partners, shareholders and the business in total).

Business Process Outsourcing (BPO)

Business Process Outsourcing (BPO) is the contracting of a specific business task, such as payroll, to a third-party service provider. Usually, BPO is implemented as a cost-saving measure for tasks that a company requires but does not depend upon to maintain their position in the marketplace. BPO is often divided into two categories: back office outsourcing, which includes internal business functions such as billing or purchasing, and front office outsourcing which includes customer-related services such as marketing or tech support.

Change Acceptance Process (CAP)

Change Acceptance Process (CAP) is a term used to describe the use of a specific process, methodology and tools specifically focused to enable widespread adoption, advancement and acceptance of business changes in organizations. CAP planning enables organizations, and the respective participants in the organizations, with the fundamental perspectives and understandings, necessary to be able to embrace business change and to be willing to commit the time, resources and energies needed to advance the change in the organization.

Change Management

Change Management is a systematic approach to dealing with change, both from the perspective of an organization and at the individual level. A somewhat ambiguous term, change management has at least three different aspects, including: adapting to change, controlling change, and effecting change. A proactive approach to dealing with change is at the core of all three aspects. For an organization, change management means defining and implementing procedures and/or technologies to deal with changes in the business environment and to profit from changing opportunities.

Communications Planning

Communications is the cornerstone of a successful change management plan. A communication plan identifies people with an interest in the project (stakeholders), communication needs, and methods of communication. Communication planning helps to ensure that everyone who needs to be informed about project activities and results gets the needed information. Every project undergoes some kind of communication planning, it is frequently informal, determining who needs to attend which meetings, receive which reports, etc. Projects of long duration will benefit from formal planning as the project stakeholders are likely to change over time. Projects that affect a large number of people or organizations may also benefit from formal planning to ensure full identification of both stakeholders and of communication needs.

Competitive Advantage

A competitive advantage over your competitors is gained by offering customers greater value, either by means of lower prices, providing greater benefits, and/or broader services. Competitive advantage is typically focused in two areas, cost advantage and differentiation advantage. Cost advantage is when a company can deliver the same benefits as competitors but at a lower cost. Differentiation advantage is when a company can deliver benefits or services that exceed those of competitors. Thus, a competitive advantage enables a company to create superior value for its customers and superior profits for itself.

Contract

A contract is basically an agreement between two or more companies, which creates an obligation to do, or not do, something. The agreement creates a legal relationship of rights and duties. If the agreement is broken, then the law provides certain remedies. There are three factors necessary to create a contract:

- an offer
- an acceptance
- consideration

One party makes an offer, the second party must accept the offer and there must be consideration exchanged. Consideration has to be something of value.

Core Competency

Core Competency generally describes the skills that a business either does well or must do well which deliver a competitive advantage. Notice that this does not include all skills that the company could do well at or all those skills required to deliver a competitive advantage. It is typically a small sub-set of skills that must be internalized for the long-term health of the business or organization.

Core Competency Map

A Core Competency Map outlines a company's core competency areas. A company's core competency areas are simply defined as those skill areas in which a company chooses to invest. Whenever a company is undertaking a change project, it is critical that it understands their core competencies; that is, those functions that the company must maintain due to intellectual property concerns, skill set requirements, legal requirements, etc... Once these functions have been mapped out, then the areas that are opportune for change become clear.

Core Competency Review

A Core Competency Review defines the areas where your company will make focused internal investments in order to gain or maintain a competitive advantage. Typically, these are areas where people work directly in support of customers.

The basic steps in a core competency review process include:
- Defining the Customer Value Proposition (CVP)
- Reviewing existing resources for alignment to CVP
- Determining desired future state
- Developing a gap assessment and an investment plan
- Developing a plan to disinvest in non-core competency areas
- Creating a change management plan

Corrective Action Plan	A Corrective Action Plan is generally used to define a process to eliminate the cause of a detected nonconformity or possibly multiple nonconformities. Corrective action is taken to prevent recurrence. Correction relates to containment whereas corrective action relates to the root cause. A corrective action plan should include a short-term fix to ensure the current process is prevented from further risk/exposure. Additionally, a long-term cost/risk weighted action should be taken to prevent a problem from reoccurring, based upon an understanding of the product or process. The corrective action plan can also address inadequate "conditions" which may produce a nonconformance. The corrective action plan should also include a root cause analysis and process change to correct the nonconformity. The plan could also include data indicating the current and future potential exposure to the nonconformity.
Corrective Action Resolution (CAR)	Corrective Action Resolution (CAR) is a process designed to document, verify, diagnose process failures to their root cause, recommend and initiate corrective actions and maintain a history of the activity. This is a key part of a continuous improvement process.
Customer Value Proposition (CVP)	Customer Value Proposition (CVP) is a technique, which articulates the differentiation for each target segment. It is a sharp definition of the value the company creates for its target customers - what it offers, the unique benefits, which nobody else offers, the costs to the customer of attaining these benefits, and the trade-offs the customer must make in choosing one supplier over another.
Dashboard	A Dashboard is used to define a reporting tool, which is typically a colored graphical presentation of a project's status or a portfolio's status by project, resembling a vehicle's dashboard. Typically, red is used to flag urgent problems, yellow to flag impending problems, and green to signal on projects on track. A dashboard is a quick and simple tool that can be used to provide visual documentation to report on a project's status to most parties that are involved in a project. A dashboard is also a means in making critical decisions at all management levels.
Driving Complex Change®	Driving Complex Change® is a registered trademark of ASIL, Inc. Driving Complex Change® refers to six critical elements: Direction, Ability, Incentive, Resources, Structure and Action. These six critical elements are the core of ASIL, Inc.'s MAX Partnering® software model. The client's input to these questions provides the Observations, Recommendations and Actions (ORA) outputs. These outputs provide the client with proven, achievable and successful change efforts.

Exception Management	Exception Management is a term used to describe a decision making methodology used to manage the multitude of business transactions that occur regularly in any given business environment. The premise of Exception Management is to focus on the critical few versus the non-critical many. This is the best way to achieve awareness, predictability and focus in the management of process activity. Exception Management identifies specific process tolerances that are then used to report only those transaction conditions out of tolerance rather than reporting on the vastness of all the many transactions and conditions that exist.
Executive Dashboard	An Executive Dashboard is a reporting tool for a select group of users. These users tend to be executives, VP's and above, the people who are the main decision-makers in the company. This reporting tool is similar to the "dashboard" but the content is generally at a higher level.
Executive Sponsor	An Executive Sponsor is the Vice President or Director who is sponsoring a change project. It is always important to have an Executive Sponsor assigned. Change requires quite a bit of resources and support. An Executive Sponsor will champion your project during executive management meetings.
Executive Stakeholders	Executive Stakeholders comprise the executive management team members that have a key stake in the success of your change project. It is important to identify the executive stakeholders so that you can focus on gaining their support and approval. Executive Stakeholders may be part of the team delivering support or part of the change project directly. They are typically at the Director and Vice President level and have the ability to secure support and resources for a change project. They are the decision makers for their organizations.
Intellectual Property (IP)	Intellectual Property (IP) is the content of the human intellect deemed to be unique and original and to have marketplace value and, thus, to warrant protection under the law. Intellectual Property includes but is not limited to ideas; inventions; literary works; chemical, business, or computer processes; and company or product names and logos. Intellectual Property protections generally fall into four categories: copyright (for literary works, art, and music), trademarks (for company and product names and logos), patents (for inventions and processes), and trade secrets (for recipes, code, and processes). Concern over defining and protecting Intellectual Property in cyberspace has brought this area of the law under intense scrutiny.
Key Performance Indicators (KPIs)	KPIs, or Key Performance Indicators, refer to specific and measurable indicators of the performance of a given business process, unit or organization that closely monitors the overall health of an function and/or organization. Well-designed KPIs are both outcomes and a measure of progress toward a particular outcome desired.

Key Stakeholders	Key Stakeholders are the managers of any function or organization who is impacted by a change project and are key to the success of any change project. They must be onboard and supportive for a change project to succeed and fulfill its ultimate goals. Key stakeholders differ from Executive stakeholders in that Executive stakeholders are directly responsible for the sponsorship and management of the change project.
Level of Service (LOS)	Level of Service (LOS) is generally used to define the various levels of service that is or has been provided. LOS is also a term used in the means of reporting and tracking the various levels of services.
MAX Partnering®	MAX Partnering® is a trademarked software package of ASIL, Inc. MAX Partnering® software helps to manage the complex challenges of Business Transformation Management (BTM), Business Relationship Management (BRM), and Corrective Action Resolution (CAR). The key function of this software package is to enable and accelerate Business Performance Management.
Medium Range Plan (MRP)	A Medium Range Plan (MRP) is typically a plan that is put together to determine the steps being taken for the next year to 3 years. Here an organization or a company will determine where it plans to make investments or where to disinvest, estimate the costs to run the business, estimate specific headcount additions, establish the goals that support the long-term strategy and determine the support requirements necessary for the organization/company to be successful. This is usually kicked off with a week long session with the management team.
Metrics	Metrics is generally used to define a measurement process, which includes the understanding of quality levels. Metrics can also mean a controlled measurement of any process. Metrics can also be a method that a business or organization develops to accurately measure various areas, for example, effectiveness of a training program, IT productivity, customer satisfaction, supplier's performance, average repair cost.
Observations, Recommendation and Actions (ORA)	Observations, Recommendations and Action (ORA) is the output for the questions that are based upon the model for Driving Complex Change® (DCC). Along with the ORA and DCC, ASIL, Inc. has blended a series for helpful hints intended to establish the framework for resolving or preparing for a given element in your change project.

Outsourcing	Outsourcing takes place when an organization transfers the ownership of a business process or function to a supplier. The key to this definition is the aspect of transfer of control. This definition differentiates outsourcing from business relationships in which the buyer retains control of the process or, in other words, tells the supplier how to do the work. It is the transfer of ownership that defines outsourcing and often makes it such a challenging, painful process. In outsourcing, the buyer does not instruct the supplier how to perform its task but, instead, focuses on communicating what results it wants to buy; it leaves the process of accomplishing those results to the supplier.
Partner	Partner is generally used to define a relationship of two or more entities conducting business for mutual benefit.
Process	Process is generally used to describe a managed sequence of steps, tasks or activities that converts inputs to an output. A work process adds value to the inputs by changing them or using them to produce something new. A process is a series of related activities and conversations, which is designed to gather input, and convert it into a desired result. By definition, a process has several key characteristics: it has specific standards which determine if it is done correctly, and which let it be repeated by others; it consumes resources such as time, money or energy; and, it responds to quality control mechanisms that can help the process be done more efficiently. A more efficient process might result in things being done faster, cheaper, or result in the creation of a better product or service.
Project Management	Project Management is the application of knowledge, skills, tools and techniques to a broad range of activities in order to meet the requirements of the particular project. A project is a temporary endeavor undertaken to achieve a particular aim. Project Management knowledge and practices are best described in terms of their component processes. These processes can be placed into five Process Groups: Initiating, Planning, Executing, Controlling and Closing.
Provider	Provider is generally used to describe someone whose business is to supply a particular service or commodity. A few examples of providers may be in the form of an internet provider, system integrator provider or managed services provider.
Quality Level	Quality Level generally relates to the characteristics by which customers or stakeholders judge an organization, product or service. Assessment of quality levels involves use of information gathered from interested parties to identify differences between users' expectations and experiences.

Quality Management System (QMS)	Quality Management System (QMS) is a term that is used to describe a complete set of quality standards, procedures and responsibilities for an organization or particular location. A quality management system ensures that your company is able to meet the standards and goals put in place, in a repeatable, sustainable and flexible manner.
Quality Performance	Quality Performance is generally used to describe the performance and measurement of the degree to which suppliers or providers fulfill specifications and to meet their customer's expectations. Quality performance is also generally used in terms of acceptability of a system or product by a customer.
Quarterly Management Review (QMR)	Quarterly Management Review (QMR) is a formal process of reporting on predetermined criteria and specifications that will provide status and feedback on the state of both parties' business partnership and relationship.
Reporting	Reporting is generally used to describe a process of summarizing data and then clearly communicating the data collected through assessment to various levels of management, stakeholders, customers, etc. Reporting may take various forms and may be done formally or informally. Through the process of reporting, planning can then be done on the level of failure or achievement and therefore enable a plan for future success.
Resource Plans	Resource Plans help to define the entire resources required to implement change effectively. There are many areas where resources are required to successfully change a function or process. Executive Stakeholders, Key Stakeholders, Subject Matter Experts, Information Technology, Finance, Human Resources and Legal are all examples of areas within a company that may have to provide resources to support a change project.
Return on Investment (ROI)	Return on Investment (ROI) is a return ratio that compares the net benefits of a project, verses its total costs. ROI is a measurement of operating performance and efficiency in utilizing assets by a company.
Risk Management	Risk Management is the process of analyzing exposure to risk, developing a plan to address the risk, and leading/controlling the activities which minimize/eliminate the risk. Risk Assessment identifies and analyzes risk and is part of the Risk Management process.
Risk Profile	Risk Profile refers to an assessment of an organization's willingness to accept risk, i.e., operational, financial, etc. for the opportunity of reward.

| Scorecard | A scorecard measures key components of performance and establishes and overall score. This can be very useful when comparing the performance of Provider's and determining Provider recognition awards. A Scorecard process allows you to measure the overall performance of Providers, even if they are from different industries. For example, you can rank the performance of your repair Providers, distribution Providers and Field Engineer Providers based upon their scorecard ratings. There will be differences in the metrics for each industry however; the major categories remain the same. Quality, productivity, delivery, technical expertise, cost savings, problem resolution and investments are a few examples of major categories that are sometimes used in a scorecard process. |

Service Level Agreement (SLA)

A Service Level Agreement (SLA) is a contract between to organizations or companies that specifies, usually in measurable terms, the services to be delivered. A SLA is a "proxy contract", a formal negotiated agreement between two parties to a service that takes the place of a formal contract, detailing the essential elements of services and quantifies the minimum level of service which meets the business needs to be provided by supplier for the client. A SLA can be used as a stand-alone document or as a supplement to a contract. It is formal as the agreed upon terms of the agreement are written in a document and this document is signed by both parties. The document is amended regularly in reflection of the customer's changing business needs and the change in circumstances.

Thus, there are two main types of SLA :
Internal SLA - a SLA between different departments within a company.
External SLA - a SLA between two or more different companies. Since a SLA is not watertight like a contract, it is difficult to resolve problems arising from failure.

Shareholder Value Proposition (SVP)

Shareholder Value typically centers on what is the value of a change project to a company's stakeholders. For example, if a change project lowers costs, then that is the stakeholder value. Other examples of shareholder value are reduced headcount, ability to scale, improved productivity, improved quality, and improved customer satisfaction. It is important to understand what value a change project will have to a company's shareholders. This is part of the justification to change.

Specific Measurable Achievable Realistic Timely (SMART Goals)

Specific Measurable Achievable Realistic Timely – Goals (SMART) is a term that is use to describe a method of setting, documenting, measuring and achieving goals.

- Specific
- Measurable
- Achievable
- Realistic
- Timely

These five components make a solid foundation for good goal setting. Whenever you are going to set a goal, you should compare the proposed goal to these five components to ensure that it measures up.

Stakeholder	A Stakeholder is any person, team or department, which is impacted or affected by your change project.
Stakeholder Assessment	Stakeholder Assessment is an analysis process designed to improve adoption and acceptance of change programs whereby the relationship of functions, groups and people are evaluated relative to their impact to, or impact from, the change program that is being designed and/or implanted with the expressed intent of creating a win-win strategy for the program and the specific entity reviewed.
Stakeholder Value Proposition	Stakeholder Value Proposition is a technique which articulates the differentiation for each stakeholder of a given project/program. It is a definition of the value the project/program creates for its stakeholders.
Statement Of Work (SOW)	A Statement of Work (SOW) is a narrative description of products and services to be supplied under contract or as part of a project generally between two businesses parties or two organizations. Change orders can be made against the original statement of work if agreed to by both parties.
Strategic Partner	A Strategic Partner is an alliance or partnership between two parties (frequently one corporation that provides engineering, manufacturing or product development services, and one smaller, entrepreneurial firm or inventor) to create a specialized new product. Typically, the large firm supplies capital, and the necessary product development, marketing, manufacturing, and distribution capabilities, while the small firm supplies specialized technical or creative expertise. Issues such as co-inventory ownership or technology transfer should be reviewed separately for applicability to the partnership.
Strategy	A strategy sets the pathway to achieve the future vision. By having a series of strategies supporting the future vision, the entire organization can align goals and objectives to drive the strategies in order to achieve the overall vision.
Success Factor	Success Factor is used to recognize the importance of having milestones to measure our progress along the path toward our goals and shows us that our primary accomplishments are the results of successfully achieving a number of smaller accomplishments along the way. These small accomplishments are the milestones that tell us when we are on or off course and when we are on, ahead, or behind schedule.
Supplier	A Supplier is any entity that provides a service or product to you.

Strengths Weakness Opportunities Threats (SWOT)

Strengths Weakness Opportunities Threats (SWOT) refers to an analysis process developed to analyze a business's Strengths, Weakness, Opportunities and Threats. The process is useful in strategic planning phases to establish areas of investment and resource allocation.

Technical Competency

Technical Competency refers to an individual's or an organization's ability to perform required technical activities, both tactical and strategic, at a level of proficiency required and the ability to maintain this proficiency as it relates to technical innovations.

Vision

A vision is a sound byte, short, crisp to the point on the desired future state, it defines the desired direction that the business is heading. The vision draws the future landscape for the organization, so that momentum can be built to drive in the future directions.

INDEX

Authors (from left to right): Peter Pazmany, Michael Vigil, Warren White